YUKON'S
TOMBSTONE RANGE
AND BLACKSTONE UPLANDS

A TRAVELLER'S GUIDE

D1729183

YUKON'S
TOMBSTONE RANGE
AND BLACKSTONE UPLANDS

A TRAVELLER'S GUIDE

Published by the Yukon Chapter of the
Canadian Parks and Wilderness Society

Chief Editor and Writer: Sarah Locke

Sponsored by

DISCLAIMER

The opinions expressed in this book are those of the authors and may not represent the views of sponsoring organizations, financial supporters or contributors.

The information in this book is intended to be used as a guide only and is subject to human error. It is up to you to make sure that you are trained and experienced in all aspects of backcountry travel, navigation and first aid before venturing into this wild area.

There are no maintained trails in this region, and backcountry travellers must be prepared for loose rock, stream crossings and other possible hazards. Also keep in mind that snow can fall any month of the year in this northern land. People must be well prepared, and ready to depend upon their own resources when venturing into the backcountry of this region.

The publisher and authors can accept no responsibility for any injury, loss or inconvenience sustained by any person as a result of the information contained in this book.

preface

Over the centuries people have been drawn to the Tombstone region for many different reasons. Two First Nations travelled here to hunt, camp and trade. For the Han, now known as the Tr'ondëk Hwëch'in, their seasonal travels took them from the Yukon River to the Blackstone Uplands. The Gwich'in travelled all the way from the Peel River country to reach this region.

Today other people also travel here to experience the striking scenic beauty of the area. They come to spend time among the soaring peaks, sharp mountain ridges and jewel-like lakes that distinguish the Tombstone Range. On the rolling tundra of the Blackstone Uplands, visitors can experience a landscape usually found much further north in the arctic.

The Blackstone Uplands mark the southernmost reaches of Beringia, and scientists come from far and wide to study the natural history of this region. During the last Ice Age, glaciers never covered this vast northern area. Beringia created a refuge for many plant and animal species, some of which are now known to occur only in this region. Rare plants, unusual insects and species found at the northern or southern limits of their ranges are found in the Blackstone Uplands. It is a landscape of unusual interest and beauty.

This guide book is designed both for people travelling the Dempster who want to spend an extra day or two exploring the Tombstone region, and for wilderness travellers who want to make more extended journeys into the backcountry. We provide information to help people plan trips into the area, and to travel safely once they have arrived at the park. Please do your part by travelling with minimal impact and keeping the campsites, trails and waters clean.

We hope that sections on the area's cultural history, geology, flora, fauna and permafrost features – among others – will help travellers appreciate the uniqueness of the Tombstone Mountains and Blackstone Uplands. The beauty of this subarctic wilderness needs no further explanation.

With this book we honour Elders Joe and Annie Henry and their family, who, along with many other Tr'ondëk Hwëch'in, have long valued the protection of the Tombstone Range and the Blackstone Uplands. We honour too Robert Frisch, who explored these mountains and alpine meadows with great enthusiasm and passed his knowledge and love of this place on to others.

Without the vision and determined conservation efforts of the Tr'ondëk Hwëch'in, future generations of Yukon people would not have an enduring natural legacy to enjoy. But, as this guide-book goes to press, the job is not yet done. Without a clear government decision to secure the future of the Tombstone park, mining and industrial roads could still permanently scar the land.

This book is dedicated to the protection of one of the most beautiful places on earth. May the wild spirit of these mountains remain with us forever.

Juri Peepre
Yukon Chapter-Canadian Parks and Wilderness Society

table of CONTENTS

maps

acknowledgements

CPAWS–Yukon acknowledges the support of the following organizations that made publication of this book possible:

Tr'ondëk Hwëch'in First Nation • World Wildlife Fund Canada, Local Action Fund
Mountain Equipment Co-operative • Walter and Duncan Gordon Foundation
The Pew Charitable Trusts • Kinnear Foundation • Canadian Parks and Wilderness Society
Environmental Awareness Fund • Yukon Government

The opinions expressed in this book are those of the authors and may not reflect the views of supporters, government agencies, or contributors.

contributors

This guidebook represents the accumulated knowledge of many different contributors, and would not have been possible without their help. Numerous people graciously donated their time and energy to provide information on everything from hiking routes to the natural history of the area. Their efforts are much appreciated.

Particular thanks also go to Laurel Jenkins for helping to lay the groundwork with the research, writing and editing; Julie Frisch for on-going help on many different topics; Bruce Bennett for pinning down those plant names; Charlie Roots for bearing with me on shaping the geology section; and both John Meikle and Tony Gonda for helping to find the right images to fit the text.

The authors would also like to recognize the contribution of Walter Lanz, author of *Along the Dempster*, who identified many of the original hiking routes in the area. SL

CHIEF WRITER AND EDITOR
Sarah Locke

CONTRIBUTING RESEARCHERS AND WRITERS
Laurel Jenkins
Juri Peepre
Louise Profeit-Leblanc
Sally Robinson
Charlie Roots
Lori Schroeder
Brian Slough

CONTRIBUTING REVIEWERS
Bruce Bennett
Chris Burn
Greg Brunner
Teresa Earle
Cameron Eckert
Julie Frisch
Tim Gerberding
Christoff Gneisser
Catherine Kennedy
Linda Kershaw
Dave Mossop
Ed Kormendy
Jack Schick
Scott Smith
John Storer
Al von Finster
Yukon Government,
  Renewable Resources
  Department

HIKING ROUTE CONTRIBUTORS
Larry Duguay
Cameron Eckert
Julie Frisch
Leslie Gomm
Tony Gonda
Rick Janowicz
Sue Johnson
Afan Jones
Jocylyn McDowell
Kirsten Madsen
John Meikle
Dave Mossop
Richard Mueller
Bill Parry
Jack Schick
Aron Senkpiel
Pam Sinclair
Ray Tucker
Mary Whitley

PROJECT CO-ORDINATOR
Juri Peepre

HELP WITH MAPS AND IMAGES
Applied Ecosystem
  Management
Helen Dobrowolsky
Wynn Krangle
Peter Long
Dave Neufeld

PHOTOGRAPHY
Al Aasman
Norm Barichello
Marten Berkman
Joe Campana
Cameron Eckert
Tony Gonda
Jim Hawkings
Catherine Kennedy
Ken Madsen
John Meikle
Pat Morrow
Dave Mossop
Paul Nicklen
Juri Peepre
Brian Slough

GRAPHICS
Birds – Jennifer Staniforth

(Some sketches contributed by Canadian Wildlife Service "Birds of the Yukon" project.)

Plants – Jennifer Staniforth
Fossils – Charlie Roots

Chief Isaac, shown here in 1898, was an important leader of the Tr'ondëk Hwëch'in First Nation for several decades.

introduction

Ddhal Ch'el, "among the sharp, ragged rocky mountains," is the traditional name for the Tombstone Range. These few words wonderfully capture the power of the mountains that we see today, hinting that glaciers played a role here, grinding and carving these peaks into dramatic shapes. Glaciers have left their mark almost everywhere on this landscape, and understanding their effects is an important part of the Tombstone story.

But it is only part of the story. It took an all-star cast of geological forces to create these mountains, including sediments laid by ancient seas, the grinding together of tectonic plates, collisions with island arcs, thrust faults, upwellings of magma, and millions upon millions of years of weathering.

If there is one classic image of this area, it is of a sheer rock face shooting up hundreds of metres above the subarctic tundra. There is no lack of drama in this landscape. But there is also a considerable amount of subtlety in the details here, and one of the keys to understanding this area is to recognize it as a transition zone, a meeting place, a place where forces come together. Its location helps explain many of the features that make it so distinctive.

The sedimentary rocks in these mountains were deposited on a continental shelf, at the edge of the ancient North American continent. To the south, across the Tintina Trench, is country that moved here from parts unknown. A series of landmasses known as terranes collided with the continent, eventually forming its western edge.

The Tombstones are at the southern edge of Beringia, a unique region that was never scoured by glaciers during the last Ice Age. Since most of North America was glaciated at least twice, Beringia was an important refuge from the ice for many species of plants and animals. Some of these plants still can be found in the Blackstone Uplands.

Different ecosystems interweave here, forming a remarkably diverse and productive land for such a northern environment. The boreal forest that cloaks most of Canada lies on the south flank of the Tombstones. Alpine flora is found in the mountains above treeline, and extensive shrublands blanket many of the mountain slopes.

Further north, in the Blackstone Uplands, stands of spruce trees give way to wide-open sweeps of subarctic tundra. In this treeless landscape permafrost has formed features such as palsas and patterned ground that are usually found far above the arctic circle.

The mountains and valleys here are home to many species of wildlife, including Dall sheep, moose, grizzly and black bears. Both woodland and barrenground caribou range across the tundra, and grayling swim in the clear mountain streams.

In summer, the tundra echoes with a surprising variety of birdcalls. Birds from the highlands, the lowlands, the forest and the coast all migrate to this area. Many arctic species are found at the southern limit of their ranges. Raptors are abundant, indicating the health of this ecosystem.

This region forms part of the divide between two major river systems. Rivers to the south flow into the Yukon, which continues west to the Pacific. Nearly all of the rivers to the north drain into the Peel, which flows on to the Mackenzie River and the Arctic Ocean.

The Tombstones and Blackstone Uplands are traditional territory for two First Nations. Both the Tr'ondëk Hwëch'in and the Gwich'in hunted and traded in this land, following ancient routes along its creeks and over passes.

The Dempster Highway makes this region one of the most accessible subarctic landscapes in North America. This two-lane gravel road, which continues on to Inuvik in the Mackenzie Delta, is the only year-round public road that crosses the Arctic Circle in North America. The Tombstone area is one of the highlights of this route.

Tony Gonda

The Tombstone Range forms one of the Yukon's most spectacular landscapes.

natural HISTORY

THE YUKON'S NATURAL REGIONS

The Yukon's rich biological diversity is made up of 23 different ecoregions – natural regions with similar landforms, soils, vegetation and climate. Tombstone Mountain and the Blackstone Uplands are in the western portion of the Mackenzie Mountains ecoregion, one of the largest and most diverse of the Yukon's ecoregions. Three major mountain ranges run from east to west across this area.

The southern Ogilvie, Wernecke, and South Mackenzie Mountains separate the boreal forest from the subarctic forest to the north. This mountain barrier also prevented the continental glaciers of the last Ice Age from moving into the regions north of the Tombstones. The Werneckes include the headwaters of many rivers, including the Snake, the Wind and the nationally important Bonnet Plume, a Canadian Heritage River.

Travellers on the Dempster Highway will traverse two other ecoregions on their journey north. The south-central part of the Tombstone and Blackstone Uplands area is in the North Yukon Plateau ecoregion. Forested valleys and several large rivers dissect this land of plateaus and small ranges of mountains.

The Tintina Trench, a wide, flat-bottomed valley formed by a large fault in the earth's crust, cuts through this ecoregion from southeast to northwest. The Trench runs for 725 kilometres, and is an important migration route for many bird species.

The landscape in the Blackstone Uplands looks subtly different from what people are used to seeing in most of North America. Vast expanses of tundra spread out to the horizons, and the contours are all smooth and rolling. The North Ogilvie Mountains ecoregion is part of Beringia, a unique, unglaciated region that was never scoured by the glaciers that sculpted most of Canada during the last Ice Age. Little vegetation grows on the limestone mountains, but long gradual slopes beneath them support extensive tussock tundra—as well as shrubs, willows and lichens.

CLIMATE

Here's a hint to the climate in the Tombstones. Permafrost, which is scattered throughout the territory, becomes continuous once you reach the Blackstone Uplands. The mean annual temperature is about -7°C, and even though it warms up considerably in summer, travellers should always be prepared for extremes of weather in the Tombstones and Blackstone Uplands.

In July temperatures can reach the high 20s, but the July mean daily temperature is 11.5°C. In January, the mean daily sinks to -23°C.[1]

In winter, arctic air masses can cause temperatures to plummet to -40°C or lower for weeks at a time. Cold air tends to pool in the North Fork Pass area.

The southern Ogilvie Mountains are a major weather barrier for storms rolling in from the coast of Alaska in the fall and summer. These mountains are the wettest of the ranges along the Dempster Highway. The average precipitation is about 45 cm every year, and more than half of that amount falls as snow. Precipitation increases at higher elevations, and snow can fall any month of the year.

The southern Ogilvie Mountains also block the warmer air from the south that produces the more continental summer weather normally found along the Yukon River valley. Dawson, just over an hour's drive south of the Tombstones, has the most growing-degree days of any Yukon community. This measure indicates the cumulative warmth of the days during the growing season.

The exuberant flower gardens and typically warm summer weather found in Dawson can seem a strong contrast to the cooler reality of the Tombstones. But the drive from Dawson City to the Tombstones is uphill and to the north. Once you're in the Tombstones, the Arctic Circle is not so far away, and snow can fall any day of the year in these mountains.

Even though travellers should go to the Tombstones prepared for the full range of mountain weather, visitors can still be blessed with warm dry days. Good weather is not uncommon, and the long summer days are an added benefit. Snowfall is rare between June

A simple tilt causes the Yukon's long summer days as well as its long winter nights. The earth's axis is tipped at a 23 1/2° angle. During northern summers, the top of the earth points towards the sun, creating the land of the midnight sun. At the imaginary line of the Arctic Circle, the sun never sinks below the horizon on June 21, the longest day of the year.

This tilt also determines the angle at which the sun's rays strike the surface of the earth. At high latitudes, the sun strikes the earth at a low angle. Instead of striking the ground directly, the sun's rays reflect off the earth and atmosphere and return to space, leaving relatively little energy in the ground.

In summer the decreased intensity of the sun's radiation at the higher latitudes is balanced by the greater length of the days there. Thanks to its longer days, northern Canada receives about the same amount of solar energy in June as Florida.

In winter, the top of the earth points away from the sun. The solar radiation of long summer days does not counterbalance the almost continuous cooling during the long winter nights. The mean annual temperature at the Klondike Highway maintenance camp on the Dempster is -7°C, reflecting the negative heat balance of this northern land.

1 *The only available weather data comes from the weather station located at the Klondike Maintenance Camp at Km 65.*

and mid-August, and the Dempster Highway is usually free of snow by the last two weeks in May. The hiking season usually starts in mid-to late June.

Snow disappears much earlier at higher elevations, and on south-facing or windswept slopes. Expect to find snow in gullies and on leeward or north-facing slopes well into June. The ice on larger lakes usually breaks up sometime in June, while smaller water bodies are usually ice-free by late May. Ice on the Ogilvie and Blackstone Rivers usually goes out by mid-May, though aufeis, or overflow ice, can linger much longer.

Travellers planning to continue up the Dempster Highway should remember that they are in a land where summers are always brief and winter conditions can return at any time. In winter, blizzards and whiteouts regularly blast the Dempster Highway. In summer, heavy rains and washouts have closed the road for days at a time.

MOUNTAINS AT THE EDGE

If you could reach it, the summit of Tombstone Mountain would provide a perfect vantage point for considering the geological forces that shaped this area. To the north you would look across waves of sedimentary peaks. The marine rocks in these mountains were formed in an ancient ocean, and have been worn down by weathering for more than a hundred million years.

To the south, across the Tintina Trench, is a mosaic of landmasses known as terranes. These large chunks of land, some as big as subcontinents, collided with the ancient North American continent long after most of the sedimentary rocks to the north had been deposited.

The Fifteenmile River, 60 kilometres to the west, formed the headwaters of the Yukon River three million years ago. This ancient river flowed south to the Pacific until a massive continental ice sheet blocked its course, forcing it to cut a new channel to the northwest.

John Meikle

Intense frost action forms these rock stripes.

More sedimentary mountains lie to the east. That leaves one final direction to consider: straight down. Tombstone Mountain looks distinctly different from the nearby sedimentary mountains because it is made of granitic rock. This dramatic spire is at the centre of a pluton, formed more than 100 million years ago when molten magma forced its way upwards.

The mountain did not burst to the surface with its present jagged shape. First weathering had to remove the sedimentary rock that still covered the pluton. Later glacial ice carved the horns, arêtes and cirques that make this peak so distinctive.

When the list of geologic forces acting on one general area includes plate tectonics, continental ice sheets, molten magma, valley glaciers, and a phenomenally long period of weathering–to name but a few –going way back in time can help sort out the sequence of events.

Two billion years ago this area was underwater, covered by an ancient ocean that at times reached inland to where the Prairies are located today. Over the course of hundreds of millions of years, a layer of sediments five kilometres thick was deposited over this region.

Most of the region was part of the continental shelf, where the waters were warm, shallow and clear. Sea life flourished in them, depositing thick layers of limestone. These carbonate rocks now form the northern Ogilvie Mountains.

In some places the continental shelf subsided to form basins so deep that oxygen was in short supply. Little marine life could survive in these cold, dark waters, and limestone did not form. Instead the basins slowly filled with mud and silica, which were gradually transformed by heat and pressure into black shale and chert.

Drab-coloured sandstone and siltstone were also deposited in these deeper waters. The sedimentary peaks surrounding the Tombstone Range are primarily made up of rocks formed in the region called the Selwyn Basin, which covers much of the central Yukon.

About 450 million years ago, lava erupted through cracks in the sea floor, building small underwater volcanoes. Some of them grew close to the surface, and limestone reefs formed in the shallow water on their flanks. Today these volcanic rocks form grey towers on the mountains around the headwaters of the East Blackstone River. The limestone reefs show up in the occasional white outcrop of limestone.

About 150 million years ago, this long period of deposition came to an end when the supercontinent Pangea broke apart. As the Atlantic Ocean began to widen, it fractured this huge landmass, and the ancient North American continent began creeping to the northwest.

The continent ground its way over the Pacific Ocean crust, at times colliding with chains of large islands lying just offshore. The landmasses, called island arcs, were scraped off the oceanic crust and added to North America.

Repeated collisions deformed the flat sedimentary layers covering the western edge of the continent, crumpling and folding them, and pushing them northward against the much thicker limestone layers that form the northern Ogilvie and Wernecke Mountains. Thrust faults separated the sedimentary rocks even further, as older rocks were pushed over the tops of younger ones.

Thousands of kilometres of ocean crust have been forced underneath the western edge of North America in a process called subduction. The tremendous pressure melted some

Tony Gonda

Glacial ice and water have sculpted the rock spires of the Tombstones.

of the deeper layers of crust, forming magma that forced its way towards the surface, intruding the sedimentary rocks above.

Three of these granitic intrusions, called plutons, form the Tombstone Range. The largest one, centred upon Tombstone Mountain, is eight kilometres across. Mount Brenner and Cathedral Mountain are the high points of the other two plutons. When numerous plutons intrude an area, they can form a batholith, which is usually considered to be larger than 100 square kilometres.

Several kilometres of sedimentary rock still covered the molten rock, which slowly cooled to form syenite, a member of the granite family. Water, ice and wind gradually eroded and scraped away the softer rock, exposing the salt-and-pepper-coloured syenite.

Long straight fractures formed in the syenite as it cooled. As the sedimentary rock that buried the syenite eroded away, the harder rock expanded, forming more fractures. Water froze in the cracks and expanded, levering off the overlying rock to produce the Tombstone's magnificent north-facing cliffs.

INTRUSIONS FORM SCENERY AND MINERALS

The huge amounts of heat associated with intrusions cook and harden the surrounding sedimentary rock. This process can create both spectacular scenery and mineral deposits.

Groundwater heated up by the intrusion percolates around the edges of the pluton, oxidizing iron particles that add brown, orange and red hues to the landscape. The circulating groundwater also carries metals in solution which can be redeposited closer to the surface.

Minerals containing gold, lead, zinc, and uranium are found near the intrusions. In fact, the entire Tombstone pluton could be considered a low-grade uranium deposit. The only producing mine in the Tombstones was located in Spotted Fawn Gulch where high-grade silver veins were discovered in 1901.

An earlier intrusion occurred 225 million years ago when magma squeezed between two beds of quartzite and cooled into diorite, a type of granite. Diorite is denser than quartzite and harder than shale. If you break off a piece, you will see tiny interlocking crystals of white feldspar and black or green hornblende.

This black rock forms north-facing cliff bands south of Tombstone Mountain. It also forms several rock knobs in the North Klondike valley between the Tombstone campground and the Klondike Highway maintenance camp.

The oldest exposed rock formation in the region is located northwest of Seela Pass. The orange-brown dolostone there has been dated at 1.74 billion years old. This carbonate rock was formed when magnesium precipitating out of seawater transformed buried limestone into dolostone.

FOSSILS

For more than a billion years, sediments washed down from the heart of the ancient North American continent and were deposited over northwestern Canada. The fossilized remains of sea creatures show the history of these ancient rocks.

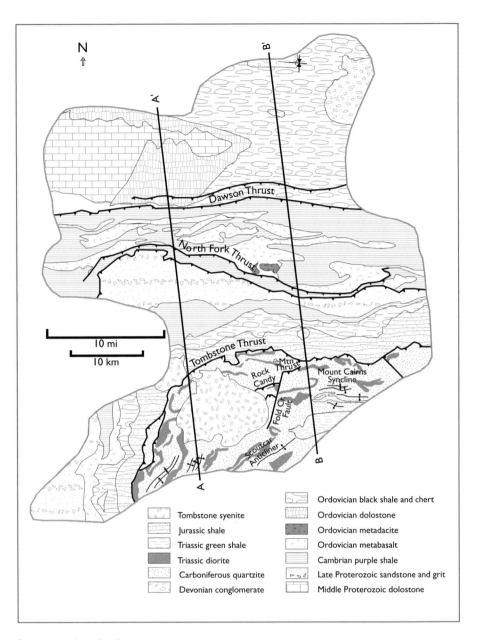

N
↑

Dawson Thrust

North Fork Thrust

10 mi
10 km

Tombstone Thrust

Rock
Candy

Mtn.
Thrust

Mount Cairns
Syncline

Fold Ck.
Fault

Scoutcar
Anticliner

A'   B'

A   B

	Tombstone syenite		Ordovician black shale and chert
	Jurassic shale		Ordovician dolostone
	Triassic green shale		Ordovician metadacite
	Triassic diorite		Ordovician metabasalt
	Carboniferous quartzite		Cambrian purple shale
	Devonian conglomerate		Late Proterozoic sandstone and grit
			Middle Proterozoic dolostone

Bedrock geology sketch map.
Lines A and B show the location of cross-sections on the facing page.

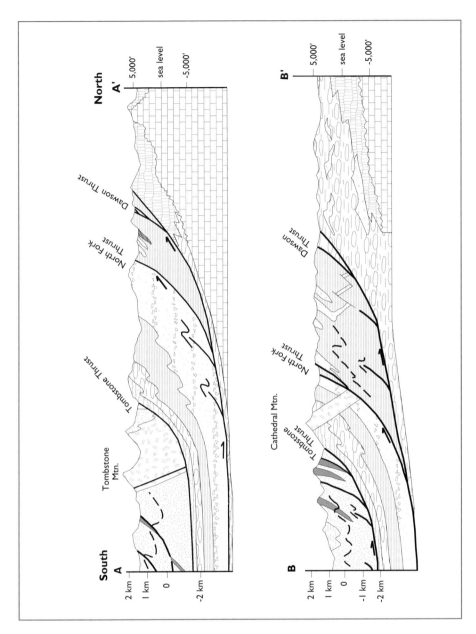

These cross-sections show the rock types and structures beneath the lines A and B on the geological map (facing page). The patterns depict various rock types (legend on facing page).

The Gillespie Lake dolostone, located northwest of Seela Pass, contains abundant *stromatolites*, algal films that trapped fine sand. One of the earliest visible forms of life on our planet, stromatolites in cross-section look like stacks of floppy hats.

About 590 million years ago, *gastropods* (snails) became dominant life forms and their fossils have been found in the grey-white limestone next to the dolostone formations. Cambrian worms slithered across the mud on the sea floor during this period. As they grazed they left behind fine tracks called *oldhamia*. They can be seen in the Cambrian purple shale, which is made up primarily of brick red to dusky maroon mudstone.

On fragments of dark grey and brown shale, observant hikers might notice curved, sometimes knobby, ridges up to 5 mm high. These are the trails of worms that grazed in the soft mud on the ancient sea floor.

Fossils called *graptolites* are found in jet-black shales. They form shiny, flat impressions that resemble fragments of hacksaw blades. Two ammonite fossils were found in brown shale near the Little Twelve Mile River.

Plant fossils have been found in the ridges south of Tombstone Mountain, which are composed of Keno Hill quartzite. This recrystallized sandstone can be recognized from several kilometres away because of its greenish tinge. Green and yellow crustose lichens thrive on the silica-rich rock, giving it this distinctive hue.

TINTINA TRENCH

South of the Tombstone Range, the major geologic dividing line in the territory slashes across the Yukon. The Tintina Trench, a continuation of the Rocky Mountain Trench in British Columbia, runs in an almost straight line for 725 kilometres from northwest to southeast. Between 90 and 45 million years ago, countless earthquakes caused the two

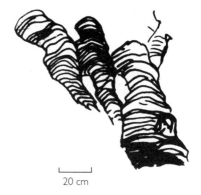

20 cm

Charlie Roots

Stromatolites

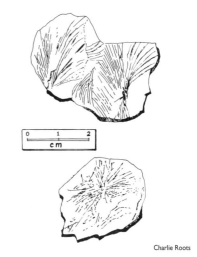

Charlie Roots

Oldhamia trace fossils are impressions left behind by worms grazing on the sea floor.

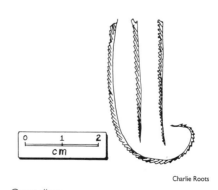

Charlie Roots

Graptolites

plates to slide horizontally in opposite directions. The Tintina is a transcurrent or strike-slip fault, as is the San Andreas Fault in California.

The rocks on either side of this long valley have been displaced by as much as 450 kilometres. Intense grinding caused rocks along the fault line to break up, and the fragments eroded away, forming the trench you see today.

Northeast of the trench are sedimentary rocks. To the southwest are the assorted terranes that collided with the ancient continent, and now make up the complex geology of the southern Yukon. These terranes are areas of land that have moved from their original locations. Some are fragments of islands, while ocean crust forms others. Often their exact origin is unknown.

The Yukon is composed of ten of these terranes. Some of them probably joined together and formed larger landmasses before they were attached to the ancient North American continent. Geologists call this process accretion.

GLACIAL HISTORY

The massive continental ice sheets never covered the southern Ogilvie Mountains during the last Ice Age. The Laurentide Ice Sheet stopped its advance about 150 kilometres east of the Tombstone and Blackstone area. To the south it came even closer, reaching the edge of the Tintina Trench and mingling in places with valley glaciers flowing south out of the Tombstones.

Local valley glaciers did form in the Tombstones, laying the final touches to this landscape. Ice carved and gouged the peaks of this range, forming distinctive features such as cirques, arêtes and horns. Glaciers ground through the valleys, dropping their loads as they melted to form the extensive moraines found in this region.

Tony Gonda

Glaciers scoured out the broad U-shaped valley of the West Hart River.

The last two glacial intervals of the Pleistocene Epoch most strongly affected the Tombstones. During the Reid interval, which occurred about 200,000 years ago, glaciers filled the alpine cirques and extended down the broad valleys, reaching the 1070 metre (3500 ft.) level in the Tombstones. The ice extended across both North Fork and Seela Passes, scouring much of the Blackstone Uplands as well.

The glaciers were smaller during the McConnell glaciation, which occurred between 30,000 and 11,000 years ago. Ice extended down the North Klondike valley as far as the Tombstone campground, and down the East Blackstone to Foxy Creek and an area several kilometres south of Seela Pass.

Only in 1996 was it confirmed that a much earlier glaciation also covered this area, changing the course of the Yukon River that used to flow south to the Pacific. During the Pre-Reid glacial interval, between 2.6 and 2.9 million years ago, the Cordilleran ice sheet blocked the river to the south and east. The river cut a new channel to the northwest that it follows today to the Bering Sea.

Neither local valley glaciers nor continental ice sheets ever covered the Dawson area to the south of the Tombstones. If they had, the Klondike gold rush would never have happened. Some sixty million years of weathering produced the rounded slopes of the Klondike landscape and concentrated the Klondike's gold deposits, gradually washing it out of the surrounding hills so that it collected in the stream valleys. Glacial ice would have churned up and dispersed the placer gold.

GLACIAL REMAINS

The valley glaciers that ground through the Tombstones during the Pleistocene Epoch left a clear trail behind them. Recessional moraines, which typically look like mounds of rock debris, mark the maximum advance of valley glaciers. One of the best examples of a recessional moraine is the series of arc-shaped ridges in the East Blackstone valley, northeast of Incline Mountain. These moraines were formed during the last glacial advance, which ended about 11,000 years ago.

BERINGIA

The Tombstone area is at the edge of a vast region called **Beringia** that extended from eastern Siberia across Alaska and the northern Yukon to the Mackenzie River in the Northwest Territories. During the last Ice Age, when glaciers covered most of North America, Beringia served as a refuge for many plants and animals. It also played an important role in the distribution of life found on both continents today.

During the Pleistocene Epoch, sea levels dropped because much of the planet's water was frozen into huge sheets of ice. The exposed floors of the Bering and Chukchi Seas formed a broad land bridge that joined northeast Asia and northwest North America. Up to 1000 km wide, the Bering land bridge was a conduit for people, plants and animals.

Pleistocene mammals—including woolly mammoth, steppe bison, lions and scimitar cats—crossed this land bridge to North America. Most of these megafauna eventually went extinct, but other species, such as wood bison, sheep, and musk oxen, survive in North America today.

Caribou have lived in the Yukon for more than a million years.

Most of the migration was from Asia to North America, but animals also moved from west to east. Both the horse and camel families probably first evolved in North America, migrated to Asia and then went extinct in the New World. The horses later re-introduced in North America were descendants of the same family of animals that had first crossed the Bering bridge.

Animals such as the giant beaver migrated north to Beringia. As big as a black bear, these huge rodents once lived all over North America.

The continental ice sheets separated some Beringian species from similar species to the south. For example, the collared pika lives in most mountainous parts of the Yukon and in northern British Columbia. The very similar Rocky Mountain pika only lives as far north as central British Columbia. Similarly, the ranges of Arctic ground squirrels, found throughout the north, and Columbian ground squirrels to the south are also separated.

About one-third of the mammals found in the Yukon today have their origins in Beringia. Caribou are thought to have evolved in Beringia from deer that had migrated north to the area. They then migrated west across the Bering land bridge, spreading across the northern regions of Asia and Europe. Subspecies of red-backed vole, Siberian lemming, grizzly bear, mink and moose are endemic to Beringia, meaning that they are found nowhere else in the world.

The valley glaciers in the southern Ogilvie Mountains isolated pockets of unglaciated areas from the rest of Beringia. These areas likely also served as centres for speciation where new subspecies evolved. Examples include subspecies of the singing vole, arctic ground squirrel and varying hare as well as a number of plant species.

Many of the Yukon's endemic plants are found in unglaciated parts of the territory, often in alpine areas in Beringia. The limited range of these plants suggests that after surviving the Ice Age, they have since been restricted to mountain tops, or other areas not recolonized by trees.

The East Blackstone River flows past unglaciated peaks along the Dempster.

Other populations of the same species survived south of the ice sheets. As a result, the closest relatives of some Yukon plants grow thousands of kilometres away. These disjunct populations are almost like separate species today.

Although Beringia was cold and dry, many experts believe that some parts of this area were more lush than they are today. They think that large amounts of wind-blown silt, called loess, fertilized the soils in Beringia and supported a more productive growth of vegetation there. The term steppe-tundra is used to describe this habitat as it is so different from any tundra environment found today. Not since Beringian times has a cold climate supported such an abundance and diversity of large mammals.

Today, remains of mammoths and other Ice Age animals continue to be unearthed in Beringia. Many have been found in the northern Yukon in Old Crow Flats and at a famous site named Bluefish Caves. Placer miners working in the Klondike occasionally dig up mammoth bones and other Beringian fossils.

As remote as this corner of the continent might seem today, Beringia is where humans first set foot on the soil of the New World. Nomadic hunters from Eurasia crossed this land bridge possibly as long as 24,000 years ago. Most likely they were following their prey into new terrain, unaware that they were making history as the first people to enter the Americas and to begin populating the last great unoccupied land mass in the world.

LAY OF THE LAND

From its rugged mountain summits to the broad sweeps of its valleys, the Tombstones and Blackstone Uplands offer a remarkably diverse range of habitats. Most of this area is

Yukon Government/Catherine Kennedy

Colluvial fans form when rocky materials creep downhill.

tundra, a treeless landscape produced here by both high elevation and high latitude. The whole region is part of the subarctic, the transition zone between the boreal forest and the arctic tundra.

There are three general types of landscapes:

- Forested valleys include the **Upper Chandindu**, **Lower Chandindu** and **North Klondike Valleys**.

- Widespread discontinuous permafrost in the **Blackstone Valley** and **North Fork Pass** has shaped a tundra landscape dominated by periglacial features, which are formed by the action of intense frost.

- The mountainous areas above treeline, such as the **Tombstone** and **Cloudy Ranges**, show spectacular glacial features such as cirques, tarns and rock glaciers.

In the **Blackstone Uplands**, visitors can easily see permafrost features such as ice-wedge polygons and thermokarst lakes that are typical of more northerly regions. Pingos – conical mounds with cores of solid ice–occur southwest of Chapman Lake.

At **North Fork Pass**, shrub tussock tundra associated with ice-wedge polygons covers most of the area. Even in areas of continuous permafrost, an active layer of soil at the surface does not remain permanently frozen. It freezes and thaws, in the process pushing rocks out of the ground and creating the polygonal patterns so characteristic of tundra areas.

Saturated unfrozen soil creeps downslope, forming solifluction terraces. Frost mounds pop out across the tundra, creating the uneven surface that is the bane of hikers.

GLOSSARY OF LANDFORMS

The majority of the following landforms were created by either glacial or periglacial processes. The Tombstone region presents an exceptional opportunity to see such features. If you think of this landscape as a canvas, the glacial features tend to be the big dramatic brush strokes. From the cirques and arêtes of the mountains, to the broad U-shaped valleys, ice-carved glacial features are often spectacular.

The term periglacial implies "frost action." Periglacial features, formed by countless cycles of freezing and thawing, are usually subtler than glacial features. Some slowly change shape over time, while others last only a season. These features add exotic detail to this landscape, forming landforms such as pingos and patterned ground that southern Canadians do not get to see very often.

The following definitions cover some of the major glacial and periglacial features found in the Tombstone and Blackstone Uplands region. Locations for viewing some of these landforms are noted in italics.

Alluvial fans are masses of sediment deposited where the gradient of a stream decreases or at the bottom of a slope. The mass is thickest at its point of origin and thins rapidly in a downstream direction. *Lower Chandindu Range.*

Arêtes form when neighbouring cirques expand, reducing the ridges that separates them to narrow knife-edged spines of rock. Ice excavates the headwalls of cirques by repeated freezing and thawing in cracks, joints and fractures in the rock. *Tombstone Range.*

Aufeis, or "overflow ice," is a German term for sheets of ice formed when overflow water accumulates and freezes throughout the winter. Aufeis often persists all summer on the braided gravel flats of the Blackstone and East Blackstone Rivers, and on the North Klondike River, visible from the Tombstone lookout. *Km 74, Km 77.*

Cirques are natural amphitheatres or basins carved out of steep mountain faces by alpine glaciers. Look for shrunken remnants of permanent ice on the headwalls of north-facing cirques where the sun does not penetrate. Cirques have formed high in the mountains throughout this region.

Cryoplanation terraces are periglacial features that occur in cold, dry climates. Over a period of tens of thousands of years, freeze-thaw cycles gradually loosen and transport surface rock to produce these step-like or table-like benches, which appear in unglaciated areas. *North Klondike Range; 5 km northwest of Chapman Lake.*

Cryoturbation refers to soil movement due to frost action, and is sometimes called frost-churning.

Earth hummocks can take hundreds of years to form, even though these small mounds of soil are usually less than one metre high. Water in the active layer, found above permafrost, expands and contracts as it freezes and thaws over long periods of time. This process churns the soil to produce an uneven surface of mounds and depressions.

Hummocks generally become permanent features once they form. Found extensively throughout subarctic and arctic regions, they occur mainly in soils composed of clay or silt that contain considerable amounts of water.

Eskers, formed by rivers that once ran underneath glaciers, look like winding rows of hills. Rocks and boulders would fall into the rivers from the glaciers above, building up the riverbeds.

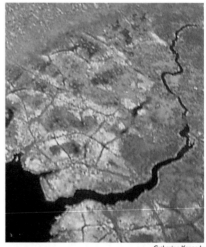

Catherine Kennedy

Patterned ground formed by permafrost in the Blackstone Uplands.

Frost mounds can form over the space of one winter. They develop in areas where ground water flows through or is trapped within the active soil layer above the permafrost. *Km 84 west.*

Ice-wedges, commonly found in both arctic and alpine tundra, are V-shaped masses of ground ice that form in the upper layer of permafrost. When temperatures drop and there is not much snow to insulate the ground, cracks can form in the frozen soil and extend down into the permafrost. In the spring, meltwater running through these cracks accumulates in the permafrost, forming wedges of ice. Repeated cracking can keep these wedges growing for hundreds of years, until they are as much as five metres deep and several metres wide. *Km 96.7.*

Ice-wedge polygons are trough-like depressions formed by the same conditions that create ice wedges. Extreme cold causes the ground to crack. When water seeps into the cracks, it freezes and expands, pushing up a ridge of soil on either side of the crack. Cracks connect to form geometric shapes, often with five or six sides.

Polygons form on top of networks of subsurface ice wedges. They can best be seen in lowland tundra environments. South of treeline, the wedges are less visible, but can be seen in riverbanks, especially after spring floods. *Km 96.7.*

Moraines are piles of unsorted rock debris left behind by glaciers. Moraines can be lateral, terminal or recessional. The debris contained in a moraine may include boulders, gravel, and clay mixed together. *Km 74, Km 80, Km 100.*

Palsas are peaty permafrost mounds with frozen cores that have alternating layers of segregated ice and peat or mineral soil. Common on the alpine tundra in the Ogilvies, they characteristically are found in areas with discontinuous permafrost. Palsas usually take the shape of low platforms, about one metre high, with irregular outlines.

Catherine Kennedy

This pingo in the Blackstone valley can be glimpsed from the Dempster Highway.

Palsas can extend laterally to produce a peat plateau covering hundreds of metres. They probably begin to form during winters when unusually low snowfall allows the ground to freeze to a deeper level than is normal, producing frost heave. *Peat plateau 200 metres southeast of campground; Km 88 west.*

Permafrost is soil or rock that remains at or below 0°C for at least two years. Above the permafrost, an insulating blanket of vegetation called the active layer thaws every summer. The layer of permafrost underneath can range from less than one metre thick to more than 1,000 metres. Changes in the climate or terrain disturbance may cause the ground temperature to rise above 0°C.

Pingo is an Inuktitut word for a conical hill. These ice-cored hills are among the most remarkable features of a permafrost environment and can range in age from 100 to 7,000 years old. Most of the 400 pingos documented in the central Yukon are open-system pingos, which are usually found at the foot of a slope.

When groundwater flowing down the slope is impeded–by permafrost near the surface or some other frost feature–it begins pushing upwards. Open-system pingos, sometimes called "Greenland type," are usually found in unglaciated valleys where glacial debris does not stop groundwater from moving downhill.

Closed-system pingos–sometimes called "Mackenzie Delta type"–are formed on flat, poorly drained terrain, often in places where lakes have drained and permafrost begins growing in the exposed sediments. As the permafrost freezes downwards, it puts pressure on the water trapped below. The water is forced up, and pushes the permafrost into a dome that freezes to form the ice core of the hill. *Blackstone Valley, Km 115, Syenite Pass.*

Rock glaciers commonly begin as rockslides into steep cirques. A constant supply of rock falling from the ridge above causes the frozen core of the glacier to slowly creep downhill. These masses of rock debris resemble glaciers in shape and movement. Rock glaciers are relatively common features in the high mountains of the Yukon. *Tombstone Campground, Km 67.5.*

Solifluction, sometimes referred to as "flowing soil," is characteristic of areas with a cold arctic or alpine climate. It occurs when thawed soil creeps downhill, sliding over the permafrost underneath. Solifluction prevents the development of typical soil profiles and influences the development of plant cover. The volcanic rocks that border Foxy Creek and Austin Pass are associated with spectacular solifluction lobes and tors. *Seela and Blackstone Ranges.*

Tarns are small lakes that form on the floors of some cirque basins. In the Tombstones, the jewel-like colours of these small lakes make them one of the scenic highlights of the region. *Tombstone Range.*

Thermokarst refers to a permafrost landscape characterized by pits, hummocks, depressions and small ponds. The melting of ground ice and the settling or caving of the ground surface causes this peculiar topography. *Blackstone Uplands.*

Cottongrass is the main tussock-forming plant in the Blackstone Uplands. These plants grow in mounds or clusters, increasing in size as each year's new growth is added on. Tussocks can become quite large, with some a third of a metre high and just as wide. Walking on these mounds is anything but comfortable and fast.

Cottongrass and other tussock-forming species can tolerate cold, wet roots. As the tussock grows, it serves as a substrate or rooting medium for other plants. Low bush cranberry, bog cranberry, and lousewort commonly grow on tussocks.

Jennifer Staniforth

Willow Ptarmigan nip the flowering buds of cottongrass. In spring lemmings and voles "mow" the fresh growth of new leaves. Some birds nest among the tussocks. A Lapland Longspur may find a concealed side cavity among the hanging foliage. Young Willow Ptarmigan take cover from terrestrial predators among the tussocks.

Thermokarst lakes develop when ground ice melts and the terrain subsides. Rain and meltwater collect in the resulting depression, forming shallow lakes. Disturbance of vegetation growing on the permafrost can trigger thawing of the frozen soil.

As the lakes deepen, they no longer freeze to the bottom in winter. The lake bottom temperature then stays above freezing and the permafrost continues to melt. In forested areas, the trees around such lakes tilt toward the water because the ground beneath them continues to subside.

Tors are isolated masses of bedrock that indicate unglaciated terrain. Taking the shape of towers, spikes or minarets, tors are formed when water seeps into cracks and joints in the bedrock, then freezes and expands, causing the rock to split apart. Many tors form obvious look-out points for surveying the landscape. As nutrients are introduced, tors support vegetation, and rodent and insect colonies. *Prospector Range.*

PLANTS

As you travel north in this region, you leave behind the familiar trees of the boreal forest and encounter wide-open sweeps of tundra. Pockets of rare plants survived the Ice Age in areas that were unglaciated. Today the cold climate controls the plants found growing here.

The Tombstones and Blackstone Uplands are at the southern edge of the subarctic zone in the Yukon, the transition area between the boreal forest and the treeless arctic. One would expect to find alpine tundra here, as this "land above the trees" is found at high elevation in all of the world's mountain ranges. But tussock tundra and shrub communities more typical of the arctic are also found in this region.

Arctic tundra, formed by permafrost and severe weather, is generally found north of the Arctic Circle. Even though extensive forests grow north of the Blackstone Uplands, some of the landscapes in this region have a distinctly arctic character.

Cold arctic fronts blow south into this region, helping to create these permafrost landscapes. Cold air tends to pool in the North Fork Pass area, deepening its influence on the vegetation.

Jennifer Staniforth

Mountain avens (*Dryas octopetala*)

Community Types

Where trees do grow, white and black spruce are the most common. Dense stands of black spruce dominate poorly drained sites, while white spruce grow on the well-drained soils found in major drainages. Aspen, paper birch and balsam poplar colonize the many burned or disturbed areas, and are also found on well-drained slopes. Balsam poplar, willow and alder colonize gravel bars along the rivers. Pine and alpine fir are noticeably absent from the area.

In some mid-elevation valleys, cold air pools on the valley floors, creating conditions in which trees cannot grow. Instead the trees grow further upslope where temperature inversions have created more hospitable growing conditions.

At an elevation of about 1200 to 1300 metres, harsh conditions again stop trees from growing. Thick growths of shrubs such as willow and shrub birch are found above the treeline. Labrador tea and lowbush cranberry, members of the heath family, are some of the main species forming the groundcover. Mosses and lichens dominate the most inhospitable sites.

At higher elevations, dwarf shrub communities form a thick cover on most hillsides. The species found there include crowberry, prostrate willows, mountain heather, lowbush cranberry, and alpine bearberry. In exposed areas, sedges and lichens form the dominant cover.

Vegetation typical of both arctic and subarctic regions can be found along the Blackstone River toward Caldwell Lake, located southwest of Chapman Lake. The wetlands of the upper Blackstone and the wet meadows of North Fork Pass are among the best places to view flowering plants.

Hardy Northerners

There is nothing haphazard about survival in the tundra environment. Flowering plants here make the most of the harsh conditions. They have developed special strategies for coping with bitterly cold temperatures, fierce winds, and a very short growing season.

Wildflowers bloom early, allowing the plant to use the rest of the short summer to ripen seeds, a process that requires more heat than does flowering. Early blooming plants usually have hairy stems and leaves that help them trap heat and resist frost damage.

Plants such as **mountain avens** (*Dryas octopetala*) and **purple saxifrage** (*Saxifraga oppositifolia*) will challenge the snows of late winter, peeking up through the snow pack. A fuzzy layer of insulation protects the **woolly**

Jennifer Staniforth

Bear flower (*Boykinia richardsonii*)

Jennifer Staniforth

Ogilvie mountain spring beauty
(*Claytonia ogilviensis*)

Seeds of many northern plants can be frozen for long periods and still grow after thawing. In 1967 a cache of arctic lupine seeds were found in an ancient lemming burrow in the permafrost near Dawson City. The seeds, estimated to be 10,000 year-old, successfully germinated after they were planted!

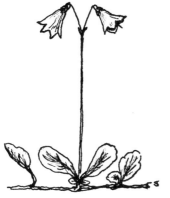

Twinflower (*Linnaea borealis L.*)

Jennifer Staniforth

Butterwort
(*Pinguicula vulgaris ssp vulgaris.*)

Jennifer Staniforth

lousewort (*Pedicularis lanata*) until warmer weather arrives. Then spikes of rose-pink blossoms burst through the gray wool.

Northern plants are generally small and grow close to the ground, where they are more protected. Many tundra plants grow in a dense mat, keeping a low profile that protects them from wind and also shelters them beneath the insulating cover of the snow in winter. Taller plants like **delphinium** and **Jacob's ladder** grow in sheltered draws.

Many northern flowers are large when compared to the size of the total plant. The concave shape of the flowers reflects the sun's heat to the blossom's centre, warming the reproductive parts of the flower. The trapped heat also attracts insects which cross-pollinate plants.

Since few plants can sprout from seed, grow to maturity, and produce seeds during the short northern summer, most northern plants are perennials. They live for many years and flower each summer.

Biennials cut down on their energy output even more by flowering only every other summer. Evergreens like low-bush cranberry and heather take yet another tactic. With their persistent stems and leaves, they have only to flower and seed each year.

Many northern plants can begin growing, absorb nutrients, and photosynthesize at temperatures just above freezing. They store large amounts of starches and sugars in their roots to allow early growth the following spring. Anthocyanins also give northern plants an important boost.

This red pigment, found in the leaves and stems of many tundra plants, can convert incident light rays into heat to warm plant tissues. Plants with anthocyanins endure cold better than greener plants.

In the fall, when the anthocyanins are not masked by chlorophyll, vibrant sweeps of red, maroon and scarlet indicate the number of tundra plants that contain these pigments.

Bear flower (*Boykinia richardsonii*) is a true Beringian species. This showy plant grows only in the unglaciated mountains of northwest Yukon, and northern and central Alaska. It's tall (30 to 50 cm) stem is crowned with a spike of white or pale pink petals.

Unusual Plants

Chapman Lake was not covered by ice during the last glacial period and many endemic plants have been identified there. Endemic species occur nowhere else in the world. Here they are a signal that you are in the unglaciated lands known as Beringia. A number of these species are associated with calcareous rock formations.

Interesting species in this area include **Ogilvie draba** (*Draba ogilviensis*). This species, common in the Tombstone area, was thought to grow only in this region when it was first identified. Now there are some reports that it also grows in the western Mackenzie and St. Elias Mountains.

Moschatel (*Adoxa moschatellina*) and **slender cliff-brake** (*Cryptogramma stelleri*) are circumpolar species, though the latter is rare in the Yukon. **Two-flowered cinquefoil** (*Potentilla biflora*) and **golden saxifrage** (*Chrysosplenium wrightii*) are Amphi-Beringian plants, meaning that they are found on both sides of the Bering Strait but not on the Atlantic side of the globe.

Arctic buttercup (*Ranunculus gelidus*) is also Amphi-Beringian though it has been found as far south as Colorado. **Ogilvie Mountain spring beauty** (*Claytonia ogilviensis*) is an endemic plant known only in the Tombstones. **Kittentails** (*Synthyris borealis*) is endemic to northwestern North America.

Porsild's blue grass (*Poa porsildii*), a grass species, is an unusual endemic Beringian plant. Unlike any other Poa found in Canada, male and female gametes are found on different plants.

Both **arctic forget-me-not** (*Eritrichium aretioides*), an amphi-Beringian species, and **Siberian phlox** (*Phlox alaskensis*), found only in North America, are near the southern end of their ranges in this area.

Familiar Flowers

Many of the flowers and plants growing in the Tombstone region are common in other North American mountains. The best time to see flowers is usually in late June and July. Please take care not to damage the tundra, and refrain from picking any flowers.

Flowers like **mountain avens** (*Dryas octopetala*), **moss campion** (*Silene acaulis*), and **bell heather** (*Phyllodoce empetriformis*) grow throughout the North as well as in alpine areas much further south. **Bunchberry** (*Cornus canadensis L.*) carpets the forest floor. Fields of **alpine forget-me-nots** (Myosotis alpestris ssp. asiatica), the state flower of Alaska, also bloom in the Tombstones.

Jennifer Staniforth

Bluebell (*Merteusia paniculata*)

Twinflower (*Linnaea borealis L.*), with its two pink trumpet-shaped flowers drooping from a single stalk, is another attractive plant which visitors might recognize from other locations.

Tall lungwort or **bluebell** (*Mertensiana paniculata*) grows in wet meadows and clearings, shady roadsides and stream banks, and occasionally above treeline. Its flowers change colour as they mature from pink to blue and back to pink again, sometimes nearly fading to white. It is thought this adaptation may attract insects only to receptive flowers. Most northern insects do not 'see' red, but are attracted to blue and tend to visit blue flowers while ignoring pink ones.

Hairy butterwort (*Pinguicula villosa*) has bluish-violet flowers barely one cm long. This tiny plant grows in the Tombstone area in sphagnum bogs and around ponds. **Butterwort** (*Pinguicula vulgaris ssp vulgaris*) is also found on damp sites, but prefers calcareous soils and is more common to the north of the Tombstone area. Semi-carnivorous, the upper surfaces of its leaves are covered with a sticky slime for catching and digesting small insects. Its violet-purple blossoms appear singly on slender, five to 15 cm stems.

Lapland rosebay (*Rhododendron lapponicum*), the Yukon's only rhododendron, is found on dry, rocky tundra, stony slopes and heathland. It grows only five to 30 cm high, but can reach 60 cm in sheltered places. In the Tombstones, the rosebay's showy purple flowers appear in melting snow and finish blooming by the end of June. The blooms have a rich, heady fragrance more often associated with tropical flowers.

Lichens and Mosses

Lichens are fungi that have established a symbiotic relationship with certain species of algae. These non-flowering plants are supremely adapted to life in the cold, dry north. They tolerate extremes of heat and cold well, and are able to absorb moisture from atmospheric water vapour. It is thought that many lichens can survive for one to several years under snow or ice.

Lichens are a staple in the diet of caribou. **Reindeer lichen** (*Cladina spp*), often called reindeer moss, forms thick, grey-green cushions on the ground. If you look closely, you will see the branching growth that identifies it as a fruticose lichen. The largest and fastest-growing of any species in this genus, it is found around the globe in northern regions.

Dzih and Dzih Tl'uu are names for Spruce Gum in the Vuntut Gwich'in language.

"Crystallized pitch is the one to take for tea. It is gold or yellow and older. The sticky pitch is younger and a creamy white colour. That one is used for infections or cuts."

Gladys Netro from *The Land Still Speaks: Gwich'in Words about Life in Dempster Country.* 1999.

Cladina stellaris grows in open coniferous forests. The distinctive shape of this yellow-green species has created a specialty market for it, as it is sometimes dyed and sold as trees for model railways.

Caribou horn (*Masonhalea richardsonii*) resembles a miniature tumbleweed. This migratory lichen has no roots, and is blown about by the wind, absorbing nutrients only when it becomes damp enough to stick in one spot for a time. Tough and horny in texture, it changes from dark brown when dry to a greenish colour when wet.

Jewel lichen (*Xanthoria elegans*) is a conspicuous, bright-orange crustose species often found growing on limestone and dolostone. It is common on rocks where birds regularly perch, and seems to be associated with high nitrogen content including whitewash from birds, urine from ground squirrels, pika and fox. This lichen helps biologists locate hawk and falcon nesting sites, and pika colonies.

Two interesting mosses found in this area grow only on animal dung, mostly on moose dung in fens and bogs across the boreal forest. Flies disperse the spores of both species. *Splachnum luteum*, with its bright yellow, skirt-like capsule base, is more common than *Splachnum rubrum*, a brilliant red bryophyte.

Moonwort (*Botrychium lunaria*) can be seen near the Tombstone campground. This prehistoric plant has changed very little in the past million years. It resembles a fern but is not considered a true one because its spore sacs are on separate stalks instead of on the leaves. Moonworts grow about 10 cm tall and are found at all elevations in a variety of habitats. The common name, moonwort, and the scientific name, lunaria, both refer to the half-moon shape of the leaflets. In ancient English folklore, the spores of the moonwort were believed to make a person invisible.

Traditional Uses of Plants

> GENERAL PRECAUTION: The following information explains the historical use of some plants found in the area. It is not intended for use as a field guide. Never use plants for food or medicine unless you are sure you have identified the plant correctly and know how it should be processed.
>
> Some people can have allergic reactions to plants that others use with no harm. Many plants can be dangerous when excessive amounts are used. Some species, such as poison hemlock, can even be deadly. Finally, many species are not abundant enough to sustain much harvesting.

When First Nations people lived off the land, meat was the mainstay of their diets, while berries, greens, trees and roots provided them with essential vitamins and carbohydrates. Many modern drugs used around the world today are derived from the same simple medicines used by First Nations people.

Spruce, the most common tree in the boreal and subarctic forest, had many uses. Colds were often treated with spruce tea, made by boiling the needles in water. Spruce sap was used as a tonic each spring to clean the blood. Tea was also made from the inner bark of the tree. After it was strained, it was used for stomach upsets, ulcers, weak blood, mouth sores and sore throats.

Trappers and hunters used spruce cambium, the soft layer just beneath the bark, as an

Jennifer Staniforth

Cloudberry (*Rubus chamaemorus*)

emergency food when they were on the trail. People chewed cambium during famines to avoid scurvy. Chewing spruce gum would sooth a bad cough or sore throat. Spruce gum was also excellent for waterproofing birch baskets and sealing boats.

Spruce pitch, the sticky resin found on the bark, is high in vitamin C. It is used for almost everything from patching leaks and holes in containers to treating colds, cuts and skin abrasions. The pitch was mixed with grease and used on infected cuts. Cough syrup was made from boiled pitch.

Willow was used for headaches. When willow bark or leaves are chewed, salicylic acid is released. This powerful painkiller is related to acetylsalicylic acid, the active ingredient in aspirin. Willow leaf buds, picked just after they show green in the springtime, can provide a healthy breakfast with plenty of vitamin C.

Teas were made from many different plants. A tea made with **blueberry** leaves or fruit was used to cure diarrhea. **Rose hip** tea provides an excellent source of vitamin C. The leaves of **Labrador tea**, which can be picked year-round, produce a distinctive-tasting tea. Roots of the **mountain cranberry** were boiled to produce a medicinal tea for stomach aches and gall bladder ailments.

First Nations people ate a variety of different plant roots, stems and greens. In the spring, they picked the new shoots of fireweed and ate them like asparagus. Later in the summer the leaves can be used as salad greens.

Berries were an important part of the First Nations diet, providing vitamins and variety.

Dried berries were sometimes stored in the stomach bag of an animal. This container could be buried in a hole in the ground, or under shallow water in a river or lake bottom.

Lowbush cranberries were picked as late in the fall as possible and kept well all winter. Also called **lingonberries**, they can be chewed raw for a sore throat or upset stomach. These tart berries contain their own pectin and are excellent for making jams and jellies. Many people consider them tastier than southern varieties of cranberries.

Soapberries (*Shepherdia canadensis*)

Jennifer Staniforth

Blueberries, **raspberries**, **strawberries** and **cloudberries** were harder to keep so they were usually cooked, mixed with grease or sometimes with fish eggs, and stored.

Reindeer lichen, also called **caribou moss**, was boiled into a tea to relieve arthritis. It was also used as a poultice on aching body parts, and mixed with red willow to produce a good medicine.

Soapberries were named for their foaming properties and bitter taste. They are an excellent source of vitamin C and can be sweetened with sugar and other berries to make a foamy desert called Indian ice cream.

The berries stay on the shrubs for a long time and are easy to find, so they can make a good emergency food for humans. The bitter flavour improves after the first frost. Saponin, the bitter soapy substance in the berries, is not dangerous in small amounts, but can cause diarrhea, vomiting and abdominal pain if eaten in large amounts.

The fruit on this spreading shrub is bright red to yellowish, and soapy to the touch. Also called Canada buffaloberry, it grows as far north as the Arctic coast. Grizzly and black bears feed on soapberries, as well as other birds and mammals.

Kinnikinnick (Common bearberry)

This trailing evergreen shrub has long, flexible rooting branches with small, drooping pinkish clusters of flowers at branch tips. The edible but mealy, tasteless berries look like miniature apples. Kinnikinnick is widespread across the circumpolar region. It can be found on dry, sandy sites in woodlands, on exposed slopes, roadsides, riverbanks and open areas.

Yukon Athapaskan women boiled kinnikinnick berries and then fried them in grease and sugar. The berries are an important emergency food because they stay on the branches during the winter when few other foods are available. They are also a favourite food of both bears and grouse.

Cloudberry

The fruit of this species turns first red, and then amber in August. Cloudberry is found in moist, peaty and turfy places in tundra, heathlands and woods, usually growing with sphagnum moss.

Cloudberries are a favoured fruit in the north, second only to blueberries in importance in many areas. However, too many cloudberries in an empty stomach can cause cramps. In the past, the fruit was preserved in oil or fat. Today cloudberries are usually cooked with sugar. Cloudberry preserves and liqueurs are a featured item in Scandinavian specialty shops.

Alpine sweet-vetch or bear root

This plant (*Hedysarum alpinum*), with its reddish-purple pea-shaped flower, is sometimes mistaken as a dwarf fireweed. It forms large colonies on grassy slopes or moist gravel flats. Harvesting this plant is not recommended because a closely related plant, northern sweet-vetch (*Hedysarum mackenzii*) is poisonous to humans.

The two plants can be easily distinguished by their leaves. Alpine sweet-vetch has prominent veins on the lower surface while the thicker leaves of northern sweet-vetch mask the veins, making them more difficult to see.

Roots of both vetches are a favourite food of grizzly bears and the principal food in some

Jennifer Staniforth

Alpine sweet-vetch (*Hedysarum alpinum*)

areas during the summer. Other names for Alpine hedysarum include Eskimo potato, Indian potato, licorice root, bear root, pea vine, wild potato and Alaska carrot, and American hedysarum.

Northern peoples relied on the nourishing roots of this plant, collecting them in fall or spring. While dry and woody in the summer, in spring the young roots taste like licorice when raw and young carrots when cooked.

WILDLIFE

Mammals

The Tombstone area is home to many animals that need large expanses of wilderness to survive. Predators such as grizzly bears, black bears, wolverine, and wolves range throughout this region. Ungulates such as caribou, moose and Dall sheep also live here, and often can be spotted from the highway at the right times of the year.

Since the end of the last Ice Age, only 37 species have migrated into the area. These include snowshoe hare, hoary marmot, red squirrel, red fox, marten and black bear. Other species in the area include lynx, mink, ground squirrel, porcupine, weasel, muskrat, beaver and collared pika.

True northern species include the tundra shrew, singing vole, Ogilvie Mountains lemming, and barrenground caribou, all of which once lived in Beringia. The Ogilvie Mountains lemming is closely related to the Varying lemming of the arctic, and may be the only mammal species endemic to the Yukon.

Many mammals common in the southern Yukon do not range as far north as the Tombstone area. This list includes the deer mouse, least chipmunk, little brown myotis bat and coyote.

Two species of bears live in the region. **Black bears** live in forested areas, while **grizzly bears**, seen more frequently in this region, are found both above and below treeline. Grizzlies are considered to be wilderness icons. While this species is threatened worldwide, populations are still healthy in the North.

About 6,300 grizzly bears, one-quarter of the world's remaining population, live in the Yukon.

All grizzly bears need large home ranges. Bears in this northern environment need even more space than their southern cousins, as the environment is not as productive. In her constant search for food, a female grizzly might have a home range of 300-400 square kilometres. Male grizzlies might require an area five times larger.

Grizzly bears are omnivorous and depend upon different foods during different seasons. In spring and early summer they feed at lower elevations on bear root, horsetails and willow catkins. They move higher as summer progresses, descending again once the berries are ripe. In the late summer and fall, bears gorge on ripening berries, an important high-energy food source. On a menu of soapberries, blueberries, crowberries, cranberries and bearberries, a bear's average weight gain is about one kilogram per day.

Grizzlies usually dig their dens in areas where deep snow will act as insulation. Bears spend more than half the year sleeping in these dens, but hibernation is still an intriguing mystery. While the animals' heart and breathing rates are reduced, their body temperatures do not decrease very much.

During hibernation bears do not feed, urinate or defecate, yet females are able to give birth. The cubs are born in January and February, and emerge with their mothers in May.

When travelling in bear country, keep some basic facts about bears in mind. Bears are hungry when they emerge from their dens. When berries are ripe, hikers should avoid areas with lots of berry bushes. For more information on travelling in bear country, see page 47.

Caribou have lived in the Yukon for at least 1.5 million years, and are superbly adapted to harsh northern conditions. The hollow hairs of their coats insulate them from extreme temperatures. Their large hooves act as snowshoes, distributing their weight across the surface of the snow.

Caribou use their front hooves like shovels to dig down into the snow for lichens, their main winter food. They can smell lichens underneath the snow. Unique among large ruminants, they can ferment lichens into usable winter energy.

Yukon Government

The Porcupine Caribou Herd regularly uses the Blackstone Uplands for winter range.

THE MAN WHO TRAVELLED WITH CARIBOU

This Northern Tutchone legend tells of a man who traveled with caribou for such a long time that he turned into one. He was infused with the spirit of the caribou, and traveled along with them. Eventually a powerful spirit helper, a Golden Eagle, helped him return to live among humans. But he remained half-caribou, and the smell of humans was very offensive to him. It took a long time for him to get used to humans again.

from *My Old People Say,*
National Museum of Canada

The Porcupine Caribou Herd takes its name from the Porcupine River, which the caribou cross during their annual migration. The 150,000 animals in this barrenground herd never overgraze one area because they migrate over such huge distances. From the herd's summer calving grounds at the edge of the Beaufort Sea, the caribou migrate south in the fall to forested areas. This is the longest migratory route of any caribou herd.

The Dempster Highway intersects the herd's winter range, and in the fall caribou can often be seen near the road. The Tombstone region, at the southern end of the herd's range, is one of several wintering areas for the herd. The key habitat in the Blackstone Uplands has better quality winter forage and receives less snow than many of the herd's other wintering areas.

The 1,200 animals in the Hart River Caribou Herd do not migrate over large distances. This woodland herd spends its winters in the spruce forests east of the Dempster Highway. In summer the caribou move up into the mountains around North Fork Pass and in the North Klondike drainage.

Joseph Campana

Dall sheep, the only wild white sheep in the world, are regularly seen in the southern Ogilvie Mountains.

These caribou are slightly larger and heavier than the Porcupine animals, though the differences are not always obvious. Animals from these two herds sometimes mingle on their winter ranges, but are not known to interbreed.

Like caribou, **moose** are members of the deer family. The Alaska Yukon moose or tundra moose (*Alces alces giga*) found here is the largest sub-species of moose in North America. Moose are browsers but occasionally graze in open meadows. In summer they often feed in ponds, dunking their heads underwater to reach aquatic plants.

Look for moose in lakes near the highway between Km 95 and Km 127. In winter moose "yard up" in areas with good browse, such as the willow thickets along the North Klondike, Ogilvie and Blackstone Rivers. Calves are born in late May. A cow moose will vigorously defend its calf or calves from any perceived threat, so these animals should be given a wide berth.

Dall sheep are a truly northern species, well adapted to life north of the Arctic Circle. As many as 500 Dall sheep live in the Cloudy and Blackstone Ranges, making this the largest sheep population along the Dempster Highway.

A lambing area is visible from the highway, but visitors are cautioned that the sheep are very vulnerable to disturbance during this time and should not be approached. Dall sheep survive in a harsh environment, and any additional stress could threaten this herd.

Dall sheep are known to cross the highway around North Fork Pass. Sheep licks are located east of the pass, and near the highway in the central Ogilvies. Magnesium and calcium are the main attractions in these licks. During spring green-up, forage plants contain a high level of potassium that upsets the magnesium and calcium levels in these animals. Lactating ewes also depend upon this extra source of calcium.

If you go hiking in the alpine areas of the Tombstones, you are almost assured of hearing the high-pitched "eeeks" of **collared pikas**. Also called "rock rabbits" or "conies," these small grey animals can be hard to spot as they live among the jumbled boulders on talus slopes, usually above treeline.

Pikas are in the same order as rabbits and hares. As these small animals do not hibernate, they must harvest enough plants to last them all winter. They cut and stack grasses, flowers and even small shrubs, forming haypiles among the rocks. Pikas are known to build haypiles two-thirds of a metre high and just as wide.

Pikas are found in mountainous areas throughout the Yukon, even among the icefields of the St. Elias Mountains! There they live on isolated rock outcrops called nunataks, and are known to harvest dead birds to survive.

The Siberian word for pika is *puka*, and all but two of the existing species of pika occur in Asia. Fossil remains indicate that the pika family is over 15 million years old and most likely reached North America by crossing the Bering land bridge.

Marmots are a common sight in the alpine areas of the Tombstones. With their short broad heads and thickset bodies, they are sometimes referred to as "tundra bears," though their nearest relatives are actually ground squirrels and prairie dogs. Predominantly gray with a darker lower back and face and a dark, reddish tail, they can also be identified by the white patches above their nose.

Marmots make their dens at the bases of active talus slopes where they can hide from predators. Most marmot dens have a main entrance with a mound of dirt near the hole and a number of concealed entrances. These social animals often locate their burrows in the same area to form a colony.

They are most active in early morning and late afternoon, and can be heard whistling loudly to signal danger. They also hiss, squeal, growl and yip.

True hibernators, marmots enter a state of torpor during the winter. They seal themselves off in their burrows for as much as eight months of the year, plugging the tunnel leading to the nest chamber with dirt and vegetation.

In the North, marmots mate in April or May. Their young, born about a month later, will disperse two months after birth. Marmots may live for five years or more.

Birds

The Dempster Highway corridor is the only place in Canada where you can step out of your car and observe birds of the subarctic in a relatively undisturbed habitat. The Tombstones and Blackstone Uplands are among the best areas for birding along the Dempster. The Tombstones have the added attraction of being just north of a major flyway, the Tintina Trench.

Jennifer Staniforth

Gyrfalcon

Using Tombstone Campground as a basecamp, it is easy to visit a diverse array of habitats. Boreal forest, alpine and subarctic tundra as well as numerous wetlands are all within range for day trips. Of the 159 bird species that have been recorded along the length of the Dempster Highway, 137 species have been identified in the Tombstone area.

Birdwatching is best in late May and early June when local breeders are establishing territories and migrants are passing through on their way north to their breeding grounds. *Birds by the Dempster Highway* by the late Robert Frisch is a comprehensive bird guide to the region. Frisch, who lived in the area for many years, was a passionate naturalist who added greatly to our knowledge of this unique region. In the Tombstones, he and his wife Julie found the first breeding nest sites of Surfbirds ever recorded in Canada.

One of the main attractions for birders is the chance to see arctic species near the southern limit of their range. Several arctic breeders nest in the alpine tundra regions of the southern Ogilvie Mountains. These include Snow Bunting, Gyrfalcon, Arctic Tern, Red-throated Loon, Oldsquaw, Willow Ptarmigan, American Golden-Plover and Long-tailed Jaeger. Some of these birds breed close to the highway. Alpine tundra also supports breeding Surfbirds, Gray-crowned Rosy Finches, Golden-crowned Sparrows and American Pipits.

ROBERT FRISCH (1930-1985)

Bob Frisch moved to the Klondike Valley in 1970, and spent 15 years exploring many aspects of the natural history of the region. He is perhaps best known for his book, *Birds by the Dempster Highway*, first published in 1982. This ardent naturalist was also known for his extended trips into the mountains along the Dempster Highway.

Bob had a particularly keen interest in Surfbirds and was convinced that they were nesting in the area, even though no Surfbird nests had ever been recorded in Canada before. He spent countless hours in the mountains searching for the hard-to-see nests. His diligence finally paid off as he eventually located Surfbird nests in both the Richardson and Ogilvie Mountains.

Bob always tried to share his discoveries with other people, and used to refer to himself as the "leg man" for all the people who did not have his same opportunities. He often collected plants for other naturalists who were not able to get into the back-country themselves. Hitchhiking –his normal mode of travel along the Dempster Highway –gave him another opportunity to tell people about the uniqueness of this region.

There is no doubt that Bob was an ideal interpreter for the Tombstone area, but he never had the chance to work at the interpretive centre, which opened in the summer of 1985. On the summer solstice of that year, two biologist friends were on their way to ask him to help out at the centre. They found him lying at the side of his driveway where he had fallen off of his bicycle. He had died suddenly of cardiac arrest at the age of 55.

His wife and daughter still spend their summers on the Dempster Highway and can sometimes be found working at the interpretive centre.

Pat Morrow

Bob Frisch was reknowned for his epic solo journeys in the Tombstone Region.

Raptors are abundant in the area. In addition to Gyrfalcon, species to expect are Golden Eagle, Peregrine Falcon, Great Gray Owl, Northern Hawk Owl, Merlin and Northern Harrier. American Kestrels have nested at Tombstone Campground. The staff at the Dempster Interpretive Centre are always keen to point visitors in the direction of the region's special birds.

The North Fork Pass is an important area for raptors. In the late 1970s, a comprehensive inventory identified a high density of birds of prey breeding along the Dempster corridor. This prompted a management plan to ensure that the Dempster corridor continues to provide the habitats required by these species. Prime viewing areas are mostly north of the Tombstone Mountain viewpoint on both sides of the highway. By scanning the treetops, ridges and open skies, one can see most–if not all–of the region's raptors.

All three ptarmigan species may be seen in this area. Look for Willow Ptarmigan in riverine floodplain habitat, Rock Ptarmigan on mountain slopes, and White-tailed Ptarmigan on barren alpine ridges. The Dempster Highway travels through one of the most important riparian areas in the central Ogilvies; Willow and Rock Ptarmigan depend on the areas within one to three kilometres of either side of the highway. In peak years, more than 1,000 ptarmigan have been recorded here.

The Willow Ptarmigan population crashes dramatically every ten years. This natural cycle is influenced by the number of predators, such as Gyrfalcons, and the amount of food available.

Pacific and Red-throated Loons, Harlequin Ducks, Surfbirds, Wandering Tattlers, Northern Wheatears, and Common Redpolls are found in the Cloudy Range, and along the valleys and ridges throughout the Dempster corridor. Tundra ponds are hot spots for many species. Two Moose Lake at Km 102.5 on the Dempster is one of the best viewing locations for many species.

The Dempster Highway continues to be an area where individual birdwatchers can make important discoveries. If you visit the area, please consider recording your observations and forwarding them to the Yukon Bird Club, Box 31054, Whitehorse, Yukon Y1A 5P7.

Amphibians

The species list for amphibians in the Tombstone area is short and to the point. Only the **wood frog** (*Rana sylvatica*) can survive this far north. This small frog, with its distinctive, dark eye mask, is the most common and widespread amphibian in the Yukon.

Wood frogs have two important adaptations for life in the north. They can function at lower temperatures than any other species of frog. Also, once the eggs start developing, they grow into tadpoles faster than any other North American frog.

These cold-blooded animals can survive temperatures down to -6°C by hibernating under the forest litter and snow. The glucose in their cells acts as antifreeze, preventing them from bursting in freezing temperatures. These frogs freeze solid during hibernation, registering no heartbeat, respiration or detectable brain activity. Yet as soon as temperatures rise above freezing, wood frogs are ready to breed.

Tiny wood frogs survive the northern winters by freezing solid.

In the Tombstone area, wood frogs live along drainages such as the Chandindu, Upper Blackstone, and the North Klondike. They are active mainly during daylight.

Aquatic World

The waters of this region are separated by a continental divide. Rivers flowing into the Yukon River continue on to the North Pacific Ocean, while rivers flowing north into the Peel continue on to the Arctic Ocean via the Mackenzie River.

These waterways tend to have different characteristics. In the Tombstone and Blackstone Uplands area, tributaries of the Yukon River have steeper gradients than those of the Peel. But at one time, the waters of these two major drainages were mingled.

At least twice during Pleistocene glaciations, the Peel's channel to the Mackenzie was blocked by a wall of ice. The Peel's waters were diverted to the northwest, eventually flowing into the Yukon River system. These diversions allowed aquatic organisms to transfer between the two river systems. Some of the fish species in the Peel River and its tributaries are genetically different from those found in the rest of the Mackenzie drainage.

The Peel River basin is a glacial refugium containing many relict fish populations. At least six species originated from the intermingling with the Yukon River drainage, or developed in situ in unglaciated areas.

Fish in the Yukon River basin are descendants of stocks that survived the glacial period in refugia in the Yukon interior. Fish also moved upstream from the Bering Sea after the ice sheets retreated.

Arctic grayling, round whitefish, chinook salmon, burbot, pike, inconnu and slimy sculpin can all be found in the Tombstone region in waters draining towards the Yukon River. These fish also inhabit the Mackenzie River drainages. The char in rivers west of the Mackenzie are now generally classified as Dolly Varden char. They can sometimes be caught in the Blackstone River.

The swift clear waters of the Blackstone River provide good habitat for arctic grayling. These fish overwinter in larger rivers like the Peel. After spring break-up, they return to small creeks to spawn, later dispersing throughout the tributaries and main streams until freeze-up.

Look for grayling in pools and eddies at the edge of rapids where they gather to feed on insects. Aboriginal people relied on these fish, and as late as the mid-1960s, stakes from fish traps were still obvious in channels in the Black City area, where Cache Creek meets the Blackstone River.

Burbot, found in all Yukon rivers, have the unique habit of spawning under the ice in mid-winter. First Nations people catch them by jigging through the ice. Burbot liver is rich in vitamin A and is considered a delicacy. Salmon used to spawn in the North Klondike River before the Gold Rush.

Insects

Insects in this part of the world have their own claim to fame, but not for the reasons that some people might think. In 1997, the Biological Survey of Canada published the results of the largest scientific survey that it has ever tackled. *Insects of the Yukon*, weighing in at about two kilograms, brings together 20 years worth of research, and much of the original interest was sparked by insects in the northern Yukon.

About 10 percent of the Yukon's insect species have been here since the Ice Age. Instead of heading south after the ice sheets melted, they stayed put and refined their abilities to cope with arctic conditions, often in interesting ways.

For example, the Yukon has a relatively large number of insects that have small wings but don't fly. Six butterfly species in the northern Yukon, including one species found in the Ogilvies, have this characteristic.

Possibly this adaptation occurred because there was not a more hospitable climate within flying range of these bugs. It made more strategic sense to reduce their wing size and save energy for other priorities, such as making eggs.

About 25 percent of Yukon **blackflies** and some of our **mosquitoes** are "autogenous," meaning they don't feed on blood. These insects probably evolved away from the biting habit during the long periods when there was not much on which to feed.

Instead they filter food out of the water while still in their larval stages. Female blackflies can use this stored food later in life to produce eggs, while blood-feeders are not capable of building up such reserves. Only 3 percent of the blackflies in the rest of Canada feed this way.

Abundant standing water in permafrost areas offers unlimited breeding sites for mosquitoes, blackflies, and biting mites. The clear, well-oxygenated streams support large populations of the larval stages of blackflies and biting mites, also known as no-see-ums.

The surface of tussock moss and sphagnum moss acts as a heat trap in the summer. About 10 cm below the surface, a miniature jungle contains an incredible diversity of invertebrates and insects.

Populations of different species of insects peak at different times during the summer. As the numbers of mosquitoes decline in late July, blackflies appear. Insects tend to emerge rapidly and en masse early in the summer here since they have little time in which to feed, reproduce and lay eggs.

The larvae of some butterfly species need two summers to mature because of the short summers in the Tombstone area. Species of Boloria and Erebia have a fixed two-year cycle, so adults are rare or absent every second year. Generally, in the Yukon, adults appear in odd-numbered years. In eastern Canada, it is the reverse.

These insects may be an annoyance to visitors, but they are one of the linchpins for all life in the north. Insects are the main food source for northern fishes. Young birds also depend on this abundant food supply for rapid growth.

NORTHERN RESEARCH

Entomologists are not the only scientists intrigued by the unique natural history of the northern Yukon. The easy access offered by the Dempster Highway has made the highway corridor a magnet for scientists in many different fields. Much of the research has focussed on the unglaciated region known as Beringia, and many museums have gathered specimens for their collections here.

Even as the road was being built, biologists discovered that a large number of birds of prey used the area. Research soon began on the Gyrfalcons, Peregrine Falcons and owls in the area. Ptarmigan populations along the Dempster also have been studied for more than two decades, and some of this work has focussed on the ecological relationship between ptarmigan and Gyrfalcons.

First Nations people had long known that caribou migrated along the natural corridor which the road follows, but the road made it easier for biologists to study the different caribou populations along the Dempster.

Some of the North's rarest plants have been found along the Dempster, and they are surprisingly well known because they are accessible. Biologists working along the corridor can always harbour the hope that they will discover an unidentified Beringian species in the area.

Yukon Government

Scientists working in a wide range of fields have done research in the Tombstone area.

VADZAIH WILL COME

Don't cry Baby choh,
The stand of black spruce
is just around the bend.

The old men are tired
of the journey.
No complaints voiced
by the women.

Days of groundhog will soon
be over. Vadzaih will come
to be slaughtered by the men.

Momma will prepare the meat
for the drying,
And Papa will play football!

Don't cry Baby choh!

Louise Profeit-Leblanc, 1989

*Louise Profeit-Leblanc, the
Yukon's native heritage advisor,
wrote this poem after hearing the
stories of Tukudh Gwich'in elders
who had once lived in the
Blackstone Uplands. In the story
a young father comforts his small
baby, who is being carried on his
mother's back. The family is
moving across the land to the
wintering grounds of the caribou,
which are called* Vadzaih *in the
Gwich'in language.*

Yukon Archives, Stringer Collection, 82/332 #56

A successful caribou hunt on the Blackstone Uplands.

cultural GUIDE

NORTHERN HUNTERS

Long before the Dempster Highway was built or the goldrushers poured into the Klondike –long before Europeans landed on this continent–aboriginal people were hunting caribou on the Blackstone Uplands. They have lived off of the bounty of this land for at least 11,000 years, travelling this region before the last Ice Age glaciers had completely melted away.

Very little is known about these early peoples, but their story is bound up with some of the most intriguing questions in North American archeology. Their ancestors were the first people to enter the New World, crossing the Bering Land Bridge that once linked Siberia and Alaska. From the glacial refugium of Beringia, these tundra hunters spread out over the length and breadth of the Americas.

An ice-free corridor between the glaciers would have allowed them to migrate south. They might also have travelled along the coast, which is believed to have extended further west during the Ice Age. By whatever route, humans had spread across the continent from coast to coast by 11,500 years ago.

We do not know the timing of these movements, and there is much debate over when people first reached Beringia and stayed there. Worked mammoth bones from Bluefish Caves located southwest of the community of Old Crow, Yukon, indicate that people might have arrived here as early as 24,000 years ago. Most of North America was fully in the grip of the Ice Age then, and Beringia would have offered a refuge for humans.

Other experts contest this early date, saying that the evidence is inconclusive. The first solid evidence of human occupation in the Yukon is about 12,000 years old. A tool made from an antler, probably a punch, found near Dawson dated to 11,350 years ago.

We know little about the ancient peoples that lived in the Tombstone and Blackstone areas other than the types of tools that they made, and the animals they might have hunted. The earliest hunters here might have pursued the mammoths that still roamed the area, hunting them with spears tipped with large stone points.

Near the close of the Ice Age, they could also have hunted caribou, moose, wapiti and sheep. The mammoth went extinct as did the horse, but later groups might have hunted bison in the area as well as caribou. Over time caribou became the most important animal for hunters in this area, an importance that continues today.

Most of the archeological work in this area has been done on sites within the highway corridor. Several different traditions or cultures lived in this area through time. With only their tools as evidence, it is unclear whether these people had always been living in the North, or whether they were the descendants of people who had already migrated south, and then moved back north again.

Sites from prehistoric times give glimpses of their lives. Most have been found on elevated spots such as ridges and knolls from which they could have watched for animals. Chips of stone suggest that they made tools while waiting at these lookout sites.

They camped at strategic spots such as Seela Pass, where they could have watched for caribou migrating through the area. Other well-travelled routes followed rivers or crossed between watersheds. Quarry or workshop sites provided them with the rock they needed for these tools.

Stories from these prehistoric times live on in the Gwich'in language. For example, Chii Akàn, meaning "beaver house", is the Gwich'in name for a mountain called Churchill Hill on topographical maps. This hill is the legendary home of the giant beaver from the Ice Age.

SEASONAL ROUNDS

Three different groups of people have used this area in more recent times. The Tr'ondëk Hwëch'in, meaning "people of the river," travelled here from their fish camps on the Yukon River and its tributaries. Known earlier as the Han, they would move into the high country in late summer to pick berries and hunt, returning to the river valleys after they had dried enough meat for the winter.

The Tetl'it Gwich'in came all the way from the Peel River country to hunt and trade here. Tetl'it Gwich'in means "people who lived at the head of the waters." Now based in the NWT

CREATION LEGENDS

Many northern aboriginal people have stories about Crow, also known as Raven. The following story is just one of many different versions of how the world and people were created.

Crow created the world out of its watery state, and out of loneliness, he created people. Crow the trickster can outsmart many creatures, including himself. Tricksters are amusing, and also creative. Through trickery Crow stole the sun, moon and stars away from an old man who kept them locked in a box. Crow wanted daylight to keep the other animals quiet. Without daylight they stayed awake all the time, chattering endlessly.

community of Fort McPherson on the Peel River, they once made their seasonal rounds in the upper reaches of that watershed.

They hunted caribou in the mountains for most of the year. In the summer they would descend to fishing camps on the Peel River. As there are no salmon in the Peel, the Gwich'in would travel all the way to the Yukon River for this favoured fish. They would trade the Han red ochre, used for paint, in exchange for salmon.

ANCIENT PEOPLES

The following traditions have been established for this area:

Northern or Arctic Cordilleran. Between 12,000 and 8,000 years ago, people hunted with large leaf-shaped stone spear points. Many large mammals such as mammoths, caribou, moose, horses, wapiti and sheep probably roamed the tundra at that time.

Paleo-Arctic. Between 8,000 and 3,000 years ago, people used microblades. It's believed that a new group of hunters from Siberia brought this technology with them. These small stone blades have been compared to injector razor blades. Set into pieces of bone or antler, they could have been used for everything from carving bone to hunting animals. During this period people probably hunted caribou and bison in a land that was still largely treeless.

Northern Archaic. Starting 5,000 to 6,000 years ago, these people used side-notched points to hunt beaver, rabbits, moose, caribou and bison in the boreal forest that had now grown up in the area. They also fished, particularly on the North Klondike River. It is not known whether these people arrived in the Yukon from Alaska, or from south or east of the territory.

Late Prehistoric. The ancestors of today's Gwich'in and Han people hunted here starting about 1,500 to 2,000 years ago. They used bows and arrows, as well as bone and antler tools. Evidence suggests that neo-Eskimo people also used the area. A quarry site on the Twelve Mile River near the mouth of the Little Twelve Mile River dates from 1,000 to 200 years ago.

A third group, the Tukudh Gwich'in, once known as the "mountain people," lived in the upper Porcupine River country. They regularly used a settlement called Black City, located at the forks of the Blackstone and East Blackstone Rivers. Their name for the Blackstone was Tth'oh zraii njik, meaning boulder black creek. For more information on Black City see the Travel Guide, page 86.

CHANGING TIMES

By the mid-1800s, trading posts had been established on the Peel and Yukon Rivers, and the Gwich'in started to trap for furs. They ranged throughout the rugged country between these two drainages, the Tukudh Gwich'in mainly using the Blackstone area, while the Tetl'it Gwich'in roamed the Peel River country. Europeans did not venture into the Richardson and Ogilvie Mountains for some time, keeping to the major river drainages in their quest for gold and furs.

The Klondike Gold Rush changed life dramatically for First Nations people. Dawson City boomed into a city of 40,000 stampeders. Gold seekers even travelled overland from the Mackenzie and Peel Rivers to Dawson, making their way through the mountainous country in-between. One party spent a winter on the Wind River where they were helped by the Tetlit Gwich'in.

The Gold Rush most strongly affected the Han, who eventually moved to a small reserve downstream of Dawson at Moosehide. The Gwich'in travelled regularly to the Klondike during the boom days, supplying the stampeders with meat and fur. They travelled by dog team from their winter hunting grounds at the headwaters of the Peel River to Dawson, selling caribou and sheep meat in the butcher shops there.

The Gwich'in returned to their traditional territories after the Gold Rush. Two decades later, a rise in fur prices brought them back to the Blackstone area. Marten were plentiful and the hunting was good.

ANNIE AND JOE HENRY

No one knew the southern portion of the Dempster Highway better than Annie and Joe Henry. Annie was born at Black City, and Joe was born at the camp of his Tukudh Gwich'in family between the Hart and Wind Rivers.

The couple was married at Black City, and eventually had 12 children. One son, Percy Henry, later served as chief of the Tr'ondëk Hwëch'in First Nation.

After Black City was abandoned, Annie and Joe lived in both Moosehide, outside of Dawson City, and Fort McPherson. But they always came back to the Blackstone area to hunt, fish and trap.

Joe Henry worked as a guide when a winter road was built into the area in the 1950s. It led from Flat Creek to North Fork Pass and on to Chance Creek. He snowshoed ahead of a convoy of D-9 Cats, picking out the most suitable route.

A few years later, when he heard about plans to build an all-weather road through the area, Joe got out his snowshoes again. He tramped out a route for the survey crews, working with them until the route was established as far as Eagle Plains. He retired at that time.

Dawson City Museum

In 1988 Joe and Annie Henry, and Joe's sister Mary Vittrekwa, returned to the Blackstone Uplands. Travelling with a group of heritage specialists, they visited the places where they had lived before the Dempster Highway was built.

Louise Profeit-Leblanc, the Yukon's native heritage advisor, helped to record the elder's stories. Joe Henry, who was 90 at the time of the trip, talked about his role in the building of the Dempster Highway.

"Yeah, they say that Diefenbaker, he build this highway. They don't know that Joe Henry he take them guys up there to survey. Even that superintendent he tell me, 'Joe you're the boss not me.' I don't know which is the best way to go that time. I never been up this way from Klondike, but just the same I bring 'em up the way I think is the best way. I take them … If they don't have me, they can't do it. I know."

When the route for the first part of the Dempster Highway was laid out, Joe Henry led the way on his snowshoes.

While visiting the site of Black City, Joe described the skin dwellings in which the Gwich'in had once lived.

"They make them round like that. Bank them up with moss and snow. They got a hole in the middle for smoke and a door flap in the front. They dig it out first and put lots of brush inside. Good house, old style!"

Further north along the highway, the elders pointed out where a caribou fence had once stood. Before the days of rifles, the Gwich'in used these enclosures to trap caribou. Using brush or logs, they would build a long fence with an attached corral. If no wood was available, they would use rocks to build the enclosures.

When caribou moved into the area, the hunters would herd the animals along the fence into the corral, and then trap them in snares set in the corral wall, or shoot them with their bows and arrows.

Joe Henry remembered the stories that his elders had told him about this particular fence, named Tthal Daii Dh'aii. "They build it out of logs. Sure must have worked hard to make it. They steer them caribou right through that way. Spear them and club them too, I guess. Never see it. Just hear about it when I was a kid."

Large groups of hunters were needed to hunt caribou in this way, so the hunts were also a time for socializing and trading. Joe Henry also remembers caribou hunts as social events. He told stories of playing football while they waited for the caribou to arrive, using a hide ball stuffed with caribou hair.

Caribou are still central to the Gwich'in culture, and they hunt animals from the Porcupine Herd in the fall and spring.

TRADITIONAL TRAILS

Long before the Dempster Highway was bulldozed through this wilderness, a well-traveled route linked the traditional territories of the Tr'ondëk Hwëch'in and Tetlit Gwich'in. Later the Royal Northwest Mounted Police (RNWMP) used this same route during their winter patrols between Dawson City and Fort McPherson.

The route went up the Chandindu River west of the Tombstone Range, and crossed Seela Pass to reach the Blackstone Uplands. Around Chapman Lake the route crossed the Blackstone River and what is now the highway. From there it headed east, out of the Blackstone drainage, over to Michelle Creek, the West Hart River, and Waugh Creek which drains into the Little Wind River. From there they travelled down the Little Wind and Wind Rivers to the Peel River country.

The Gwich'in relied on key landmarks to find their way. A hill ringed by spruce trees, located between the Yukon and Blackstone Rivers, was called Ts'ok iitl'in, which means "spruce standing in an arc." This feature stood out on the largely treeless tundra. Once a caribou surround was built near it.

The RNWMP followed this same route when they began patrolling between their posts at Dawson, Fort McPherson and Herschel Island in the winter of 1904-05. The police con-

The Tr'ondëk Hwëch'in followed traditional trails through this region long before the day of the Gold Rush.

sidered the 765-kilometre route, which took about fifty days, to be very difficult, but only one patrol came to grief.

The "Lost Patrol" disaster occurred in the winter of 1910-11. Traveling southwest from Fort McPherson without a native guide, a patrol led by Insp. F.J. Fitzgerald lost its way near the headwaters of the Little Wind River. The patrol was also short of food, so they attempted to return to Fort McPherson but exhaustion and hunger stopped them.

Constables Kinney and Taylor died about 55 kilometres from the town. Insp. Fitzgerald and ex-Constable Carter made it only another 15 kilometres before perishing. From that time on, all patrols were required to have a native guide with them. The patrols ended in 1921.

WILDERNESS CABINS

The remains of a number of cabins are still scattered around the area. White trappers, attracted to the area by good trapping conditions and fur prices, built a number of cabins, including one on the east side of the Upper Blackstone River.

Prospectors, perhaps frustrated by their lack of luck in the Klondike, searched the area for mineral wealth. They came looking for gold and silver hardrock prospects. The only mine that ever produced ore was located in Spotted Fawn Gulch off of the Little Twelve Mile drainage. It was mined in the 1920s.

The oldest cabin in the upper Blackstone area, located at the northeast end of Seela Pass, once belonged to a Tukudh Gwich'in elder named Old Man Michelle who lived there in the early 1900s. Gwich'in people continued to use the cabin when travelling between Moosehide and the Peel River. Between 1905 and 1912, Royal Northwest Mounted Police

(RNWMP) patrols also stopped there on their way to Fort McPherson.

Before 1928, the families of Joe and Annie Henry and Mary Vittrekwa used to travel regularly between the Blackstone country and a prominent mountain, T'schejou or Log Cabins Place, at the headwaters of the Ogilvie River. There were at least six tent houses there. They were erected on log bases similar to those used at Black City. Joe Henry remembers T'schejou as the site of a caribou surround.

Some of the existing cabins in this area belong to wood cutters or trappers. It is recommended that campers not stay in any of these structures as a precaution against the hanta virus.

CORPORAL DEMPSTER

The Dempster Highway is named after RNWMP officer W.J.D. Dempster, who led the search for the Lost Patrol. Born in Wales in 1876, Jack Dempster came to Canada in 1897 and immediately joined the RNWMP. He was transferred to the Yukon in 1898, and by 1911 was a renowned bushman and musher.

Corporal Dempster left Dawson to search for the missing men after it was clear that they were overdue. His party covered the route in record time, despite storms and bad weather. They picked up the lost patrol's snow-covered trail on the Little Wind River and found the bodies of Fitzgerald and his three companions. The officers were buried in Fort McPherson.

Jack Dempster gave "outstanding service" to the Yukon for 37 years. He retired to Vancouver with the rank of inspector in 1934 and died in 1964.

Dawson City Museum, 984-76-2

Corporal Dempster, shown here on the right, lead the search party which eventually found the remains of the Lost Patrol.

THE YUKON DITCH

One of the Yukon's most ambitious industrial projects ever was built in this area. The huge dredges used to mine the creeks near Dawson required large quantities of water and electricity, so in 1906, work started on the Yukon Ditch. It took three summers to complete this system of flumes, pipes and siphons, which brought water 112 kilometres from the Ogilvie Mountains to the Klondike Gold Fields. A hydroelectric power plant in the Little Twelve Mile Valley supplied the power for the dredges.

At its peak, the company operating the ditch employed more than 1,000 men and delivered 55,000 gallons of water per minute. In 1933, the Yukon Consolidated Gold Corp. took over the assets of the Yukon Gold Co. and shut down operations on the ditch. The northern portions of the ditch can still be seen, though they have fallen into ruin.

MOVING WATER WITHOUT PUMPS

The ditch gradually dropped in elevation along its route. Wooden flumes fed the water into boxes at the top end of wooden or steel pipes. Where the water had to travel from one valley to the next, inverted siphons were used to create the volume and pressure needed to push the water up to the next ridge. Pressure boxes at the lower end of the siphon transferred the water back into a flume. Simple ditches were used on flat ground.

Maintenance camps were located every 15-20 kilometres for "ditchwalkers" who repaired leaks and kept the flume level. The large complex at the Little Twelve Mile Power Plant housed both single men and families. The twenty-four buildings there included tool and storage sheds, bunk houses, a mess hall, a tin powder shed and a collapsed barn. This substantial community even had an underground water system for fire protection, wooden boardwalks and a shower.

Nineteen sites or cabins can be reached within a day or two hike from the Little Twelve Mile Power Plant Complex. A road follows the Twelve Mile River from the power plant to Kentucky Point, where a maintenance camp was located with two bunkhouses, a barn and a blacksmith shop.

The ditch along this route is relatively untouched and the abandoned structures are in fairly good condition. Nine men lived at another maintenance camp at Slate Creek where there was a stores building, greenhouse, mess hall and a bunkhouse. Approximately 460 m (1500 ft) north of the camp is a forge shed and log winch shed. A tram line crosses the flume here.

Water for the Yukon Ditch was diverted from the Tombstone River. A log cabin with a collapsed sod roof located at the intake was a watchman's cabin. There is no road to the cabin and supplies would have arrived on a winter road or been "trundled" along the top of the flume. The ditchwalker could bring in a small amount of supplies in a small wheelbarrow-like cart pushed along a board on the top of the flume.

The Yukon Ditch carried water 112 kilometres south to the Klondike Gold Fields.

traveller's
GUIDE

WILDERNESS EXPERIENCE

Only experienced wilderness travellers should consider a backcountry trip into this remote area. There are no established trails in the Tombstones or Blackstone Uplands, and hikers must rely on their own resources and route-finding abilities.

People sometimes come to the Tombstones unprepared for the cold and/or the lack of trails. Plan ahead so that you can fully enjoy and appreciate this unique area. It's well worth the effort.

SEASONAL CYCLE

Not many people visit the Tombstones in winter because it is just too cold and dark during this season. Starting around March, skiers do tour in the backcountry. The Tombstones are not noted for great powder skiing, and snow conditions can be very variable.

Most years the hiking season starts in mid-June. Travel across the remaining wind-packed snow can be easier at this time than in mid-summer when hikers must contend with head-high bushes. July is the best month for alpine wildflowers, and for long days under the midnight sun. These attractions can balance out the annoyance of the bug season.

The Tombstones come into their true glory in the autumn, which begins in August. The fall colours here are extraordinary. The hillsides are painted with sweeps of scarlet and maroon, set off by the yellow, orange and green of the deciduous trees. Early frosts kill off the biting insects.

STREAM CROSSINGS

Here are a few tips for crossing streams:

- Don't cross barefoot. Wear an old pair of running shoes while crossing streams.
- Use a sturdy stick for support and for testing water depth. Plant the stick upstream when crossing.

- Move across the stream in a diagonal fashion, facing upstream.

- Always undo waist and chest straps on your pack for easy removal in case you fall.

If a stream crossing looks too risky, turn back and find another route.

EMERGENCY HELP

Hikers must be self-reliant as there are no rangers or backcountry patrols in the Tombstone area. If outside help is needed in an emergency, there are radiophones at both the Dempster Interpretive Centre and the highway maintenance camp at Km 65.

Al Aasman

Hiker making a brew on Glissade Pass. Even in summer, travellers should be prepared for all types of weather.

MAPS

Topographic maps are available in Whitehorse at Mac's Fireweed Bookstore on Main Street. In Dawson check for maps at Fischer Contracting, 10 km east of Dawson on the Klondike Highway. Maps are sometimes sold at the interpretive centre at the Tombstone campground, and are also available by mail from the Canada Map Office, 615 Booth St., Ottawa, Ontario, K1A 0E8.

Topographic maps for this area are: 1:250,000-Dawson 116 B & 116 C; 1:50,000-Tombstone River 116 B/7; Upper Klondike River 116 B/8; North Fork Pass 116 B/9; and Seela Pass 116 B/10.

WATER QUALITY

Giardia has been documented in the North Klondike River, and it could well exist in popular lakes such as Grizzly and Divide. Hikers must use their own judgment on whether to boil, filter or otherwise purify the water. Check with staff at the interpretive centre for current information.

FOOD AND EQUIPMENT

Wear a sturdy pair of hiking boots with a strong shank in the Tombstones. You will need them when crossing scree slopes and boulder fields. The ideal boots for this area would not have an overly heavy lug sole as pronounced treads tear up the fragile tundra vegetation.

You need to bring clothing for warm, cold and wet conditions. You never know which air mass will win the atmospheric war in this area, so be prepared for any and all types of summer weather.

In Whitehorse you can buy all the necessary food and equipment for a backcountry trip. Dawson City also has well-stocked grocery stores.

INSECTS

Here's the good news. No cases of malaria have been reported this far north. But even if they do not normally carry diseases, biting insects do thrive in the Tombstone region. From mid-June to mid-July, humans may evade this annoyance on high ridges but in the valley bottoms, bug jackets and/or head nets are recommended equipment. Remember that insects are attracted to carbon dioxide. Some experienced hikers swear that staying calm, thus lowering the amount of carbon dioxide that you exhale, makes you a less attractive target.

BEARS

Grizzly bears are more common in the Tombstone region than black bears. Grizzlies are an "umbrella" species, an indicator of the integrity of natural systems. The presence of these animals shows that this landscape is still wild and healthy.

The bears in this area are not yet used to humans, and wild bears will normally avoid people. When people have been charged by grizzlies, it is usually because they surprised the bear. To date, there have been no reports of any maulings in the Tombstone area. Please ensure that you make every effort to maintain this record. Always remember that you are venturing into the grizzlies' home range, and must act appropriately.

Most grizzly attacks occur when people surprise bears. Many of the hiking routes in the Tombstones pass through thick brush where visibility is not good. Make lots of noise when you cannot see where you are going, or what might be headed your way.

Bears spend most of their time looking for food. Stay away from areas with lots of berry bushes when the berries are ripe. If you spot fresh signs of bear diggings—such as over-turned rocks or dug-up ground—leave the area. If you see carrion, leave immediately. Bears are scavengers and could be nearby.

Carrying bear spray is advised, though it is not a substitute for prevention. Bear sprayers are available at outdoor stores in Whitehorse and Dawson City. Pay close attention to the directions. Carry the spray where it is immediately available. You will not have time to take it out of your pack in a surprise encounter.

Bear spray is only effective when used at close range since red pepper, the active ingredient in the spray, must make contact with the bear's eyes or nose. Bears are attracted to strong smells so never use the spray like mosquito repellent, applying it to your tent or clothing. The scent could attract bears.

Tourism Yukon distributes a booklet entitled *Into the Yukon Wilderness* that covers most aspects of wilderness travel. A section of the book describes prevention techniques and what to do if you encounter a bear. The booklet is available at the Visitor Reception Centre in Whitehorse, or you can request it from Tourism Yukon at Box 2703, Whitehorse, Yukon. Y1A 2C6. Phone (867) 667-5340.

Knowledge is power. Take the time to learn about bear behaviour and habits so that you can decrease the chance of an encounter. You will also be better prepared if you do encounter a bear.

If you see a bear, leave the area, detour around the bear or wait until it leaves. If you can't avoid the bear, alert it to your presence by moving upwind so that it can smell you. Wave your arms and talk in a calm but firm voice so that it knows you are human.

If a grizzly bear approaches you or you surprise one, some general rules of thumb are:

- Talk in a calm voice and back away from the bear.
- Do not run as the bear may chase you.
- If the bear keeps following you, stand your ground and group together to present a stronger front.
- If you're carrying bear spray, check the wind direction and be ready to use it.
- Try to determine whether the bear is seeking food or acting in self-defence (protecting cubs or a carcass).

If the grizzly bear attacks:

- Play dead if the bear seems to be acting in self-defence, but not until the bear makes contact.
- Fight back if the bear seems to view you as food. This behaviour is more typical of black bears, but in rare cases grizzlies have also predated on humans.
- If you are forced to fight, fight hard. Kick, punch or hit the bear with whatever is available. Aim for its sensitive nose.

If you encounter a female grizzly with cubs, remember that she primarily wants to ensure that you are not a threat.

Remember that prevention is better than confrontation. Here are some generally accepted suggestions for avoiding encounters with bears:

- Travel in a group if possible. A grizzly has never attacked a party with a minimum of six people.
- Cook and store food well away from your camp.
- If available, carry and store your food in a bear-proof container.
- Minimize the odours of trip food. Leave the sardines at home.
- Stay away from carrion as a bear might be nearby.

Yukon Government

Grizzly bears travel huge distances in their constant search for food.

The following recommendation falls into the "who knows if it works, but it can't hurt" category. Some people routinely pee on the ground around their tents, scent-marking their territory as would the family dog. The hope is that bears will pick up on the unfamiliar scent and avoid the area. It is not known whether this theory has ever been scientifically tested.

Be bear aware, but remember that grizzly attacks are very rare, particularly when the bears are wild. Staff at the Dempster Interpretive Centre can give you information about recent reportings of bears in the area.

In late summer bears are often seen feeding on slopes across the highway from the Tombstone campground. These bears are still wild; they are not so-called "problem bears" looking for human food. When they do move close to the campground, it is usually to feed on berries, and the campground is closed until they vacate the area.

Campers must take precautions to ensure that these bears do not become used to humans. Store your food carefully, and put garbage in the bear-proof receptacles.

"LEAVE NO TRACE" WILDERNESS TRAVEL

We always have an impact on the environment when we travel into the backcountry. Whenever we visit a wild place like the Tombstones, we leave behind signs of our passage. The aim of all "Leave No Trace" (LNT) programs is to make those traces as faint as possible.

Visitors may think that the Tombstone and Blackstone Uplands appear rugged, but this is actually a fragile environment. Plants grow slowly, and scars take many years to heal. We must ensure that we don't damage the land during our visits.

You can think of treading lightly in this land as a challenge. What can you do to leave the land in at least as good of shape as you found it? The Yukon is one of the wildest places left on the continent, and the Tombstone region is one of its jewels. Take good care of it.

Many fine books describing minimum impact wilderness travel are available for travellers who want the latest information. If you are in doubt about how to care for the land during your trip, ask staff at the Dempster Interpretive Centre for advice. Always err on the side of caution for the environment. The following tips give some ideas on how to travel with respect for the land and its inhabitants.

Campsites

Durability is the most important consideration when choosing a campsite. Avoid pitching your tent on fragile plant communities. If possible, choose unvegetated ground for your camp. The next best choice would be resilient vegetation such as grasses, sedges and kinnikinnik.

In popular locations such as Grizzly, Talus and Divide Lakes, use any obvious camp spots rather than creating new ones. Try to leave the site as natural as possible. If you do not have a free-standing tent, use good quality tent pegs rather than ripping rocks out of the ground.

Choose a durable spot for your kitchen, and minimize trampling by wearing soft-soled shoes. Avoid walking the same route over and over as you may create a permanent trail.

Please be aware that animals also depend on these lakes. Avoid camping near sensitive wildlife habitat such as major wildlife trails, mineral licks or bird nesting areas. The major lakes are always an attraction for campers. During berry season, avoid camping near large patches of berry bushes that might be frequented by bears.

Always remember that you are in bear country. Your kitchen should be well away from and downwind of your tent site. Keep a clean campsite, and store your food well away from tenting and cooking areas.

In alpine areas, the recommended technique of hanging your food bag on a line between two trees is not possible. A more viable alternative is to carry a bear-resistant food container. These canisters are already required equipment when backpacking in Kluane National Park.

Soap and Shampoo

Avoid using soap and shampoo in the wilderness. If you must use them, use a biodegradable type in small amounts. Rinse soap and shampoo residue well away from sources of water.

Campfires

Campfires are still acceptable in most parts of the Yukon, but not in this region. Trees grow too slowly in this area to replenish the wood supply, so campfires should only be built in emergencies. Take along a camping stove for cooking. If you are forced to build a fire, make sure that you leave no trace of it.

Garbage

It's simple. If you can carry it in, you can carry it out. Careful packing before your trip will make life easier. Try to remove excess packaging and small, easily lost things such as transparent candy wrappers. Make sure you "sweep" your campsite visually before you leave to ensure you haven't overlooked small items such as twist ties.

Human Waste

This topic deserves every hiker's care and consideration. Almost nothing can destroy a wilderness experience more quickly than stumbling upon someone else's poop next to a campsite, or finding toilet paper peeping out from under rocks. If feces pollute the water table, they can also cause Giardia, or beaver fever.

Please be responsible, and keep three goals in mind when going to the wilderness "bathroom":

Ken Madsen

Camping stoves, not campfires, are the standard for backcountry travel in this area.

- minimize the risk of water pollution
- minimize the risk of others stumbling upon it
- maximize the rate of decomposition if possible.

The recommended method in the Tombstones is to use a shallow "cat hole."

Pick an out-of-the-way patch of tundra, well away from campsites and water. Peel back a small patch of surface vegetation, and dig a hole with the heel of your boot. Replace this vegetation afterwards to cover the hole. If sphagnum moss is available, it can do double duty as toilet paper, and you won't have to worry about what to do with it afterwards.

If you are near an area of scree, you might consider excavating some rocks to make the hole. Be sure to replace them afterwards.

Ideally toilet paper should be carried out. Never bury your toilet paper as animals might dig it up. Another disposal method is to burn carefully the toilet paper in the cat hole. This method is only suggested for non-forested areas where there is a minimal fire hazard.

Do not build a fire, just ignite the toilet paper itself, and make sure that it is thoroughly burned. Ensure that no fire is left smoldering in the hole. Always pack out sanitary napkins and tampons, and any unburned toilet paper.

Latrines should only be used if you are travelling with a large group or are planning a long stay at one site. Problems with latrines include disturbed soil, slow rate of decomposition, high possibility of pollution and an increased chance that animals will dig up the contents. Locate latrines at least 150 metres from water and dig a hole 20-30 centimetres deep. Try to remove the vegetation and soil on the top as a single unit and replace it later. Sprinkle soil on the top after each use.

Make sure you leave a clean camp. Human foods are not necessarily healthy for animals.

Leftover foods can be carried out. Sieve dishwater to remove any bits of food and carry them out as well.

Hunting and Fishing

You need a licence to hunt or fish in the Yukon. Permits are available in Dawson City as well as Whitehorse. For more information call the Yukon Department of Renewable Resources in Whitehorse at 667-5110. Outside Whitehorse call toll-free at 1-800-661-0408, extension 5110.

Along with your permit, you will receive a summary of the territorial regulations on hunting and/or fishing. Please ensure that you follow them, and are extra careful about not over-fishing as fish mature more slowly in these northern waters.

Wildlife Viewing

One of the attractions of the Tombstone region is its healthy wildlife populations. Just knowing that a region is home to grizzly bears, caribou and Dall sheep can make the land seem more alive. Even if you don't see wildlife, you know that you are visiting a place that is still wild.

Please remember that seeing wildlife is a privilege. If you treat animals with respect, you can help make any encounter a positive one for all species involved. Use common sense and good judgement to preserve the Yukon's natural heritage for future generations.

By learning about the behaviour and sensitivity of each wildlife species, we can be better stewards of wildlife and their habitat. Confine your movements wherever possible to designated trails and viewing platforms, found along the highways. Avoid harassing or feeding wildlife. Help keep the wild in wildlife!

Avoid nesting sites and dens. Never touch or feed wild animals. Baby animals are seldom orphaned or abandoned, and it is against the law to take them away.

Be cautious about hiking on animal trails. In thick bush you may have a close encounter that would be best avoided. It is best to "get close" to wildlife with binoculars, spotting scopes and telephoto lenses rather than by approaching too near. Animals need to put on fat during the brief northern summer. Spooked animals burn precious energy reserves.

Pets hinder wildlife viewing because they may chase, injure or kill wild animals. Control your pets or leave them at home.

John Meikle

Wildlife viewing from the Dempster Highway.

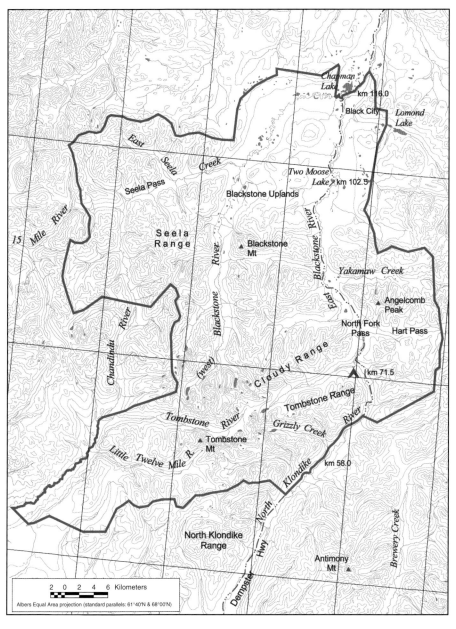

Tombstone Territorial Park boundary announced December 9, 1999. (See regional map on p. 127, and relief map on p. 128.)

Fall colours at Divide Lake

Paul Nicklen

Blueberry harvest

Tony Gonda

Moss gardens above Grizzly Lake

Blackstone Uplands

Snowshoe hare in locoweed

Tony Gonda

Mount Monolith

Paul Nicklen

Peregrine Falcon

Tony Gonda

Hiking above Grizzly Lake

Paul Nicklen

Long-tailed Jaeger

Paul Nicklen

Grizzly bear, the icon of true wilderness

Yukon Government

Fall colours in the North Klondike River valley

Al Aasman

Instant refreshment

John Meikle

Purple cress

Juri Peepre

Alpine forget-me-nots

Tony Gonda

Fields of arrowleaf senecio

Golden draba

Jewel lichen

Bistort

Camping under the midnight sun

Hoary marmot

Fall colours highlight the tundra

Weasel

Pat Morrow

Talus Lake

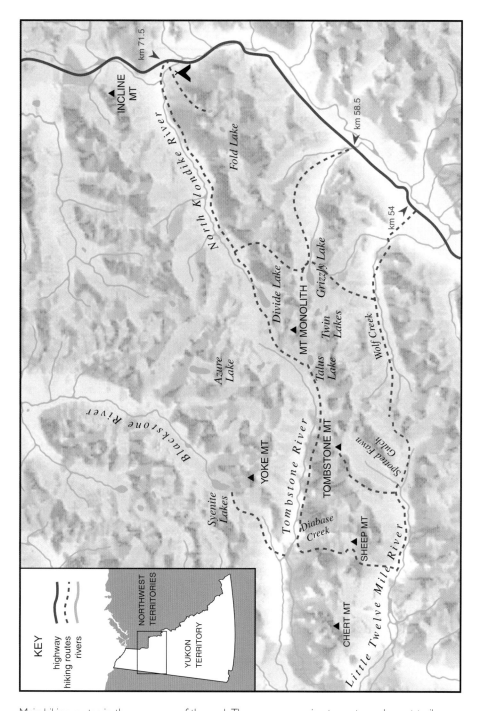

Main hiking routes in the core area of the park. These are approximate routes only – not trails.

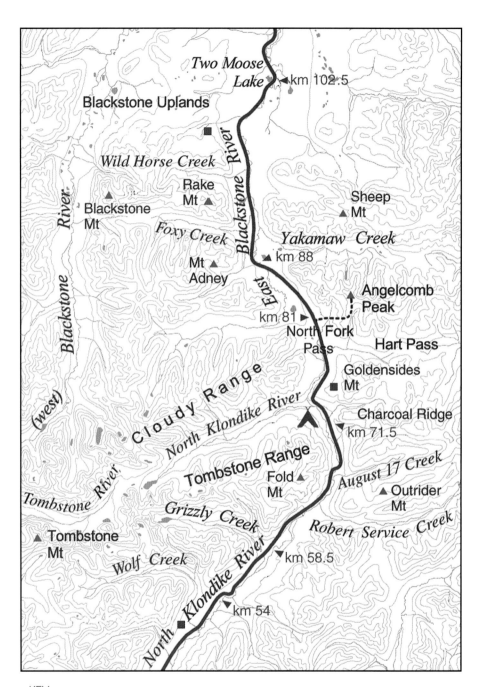

Two Moose Lake ◀km 102.5

Blackstone Uplands

■

Wild Horse Creek

Blackstone River

Rake
Mt ▲

▲ Blackstone
Mt

Sheep
▲ Mt

Foxy Creek

Yakamaw Creek

◀▲ km 88

Mt ▲
Adney

East

Angelcomb
Peak

km 81 ▶   ┆
┌----------┘
North Fork
Pass

Hart Pass

Goldensides
■ Mt

C l o u d y   R a n g e

North Klondike River

(west)

Blackstone River

ᐱ

Charcoal Ridge

▼ km 71.5

Tombstone Range

August 17 Creek

Tombstone River

Fold ▲
Mt

▲ Outrider
Mt

Grizzly Creek

Robert Service Creek

▲ Tombstone
Mt

Wolf Creek

North Klondike River

▼ km 58.5

North Klondike River

▼ km 54

■

KEY

■   microwave tower

ᐱ   Tombstone Territorial Park Campground (see also p. 128)

Highway Map

tombstone
AND BLACKSTONE UPLANDS

This guide has information for different types of travelers. The first section covers the highway corridor, and has details both on day hikes and interesting features along the road. You could happily spend weeks just taking day trips in this region. Numerous peaks and ridges are close to the road, and their summits offer fantastic views in all directions.

The travel guide also indicates points-of-interest along the highway, usually tied to the unique natural and cultural history of the area (refer to highway map, page 68). In few places in North America can such an assortment of permafrost features be seen next to a highway, so it is worth stopping and taking the time to investigate these landforms.

A second section offers information on backcountry routes in this region. Hiking through the dramatic scenery and wild lands in this region can be exhilarating, but a reality-check must also be offered. There are almost no established trails in this area. On a very few of the most popular routes, some sections of trail can be found. But in general hiking in this area can be challenging, and can test people's route-finding abilities.

The Tombstone Campground is located right at the transition between the boreal forest to the south and the tundra to the north. Most people prefer day hikes north of the campground, where the routes are all above treeline. South of the Tombstone campground, hikers must be prepared to push through the forest for some distance before reaching the alpine tundra. Grizzly Valley is the only route south of the campground with any sort of a trail.

The Tombstone Range is infamous for the thick brush at lower elevations. In most of the major drainages, hikers must choose between battling bushes in the valley bottoms, sidehilling across steep slopes or climbing high to a dry ridge. When possible, climbing high is usually the best choice.

Further north, the tundra can present its own set of challenges. Walking across hummocks, tussocks and soft ground can be surprisingly slow. The tundra can also distort your sense of distance. Without trees as reference points, a fairly long distance may appear quite short.

Where the Dempster Highway parallels the East Blackstone River, hikers have a choice of obstacles. To the west, they must cross one or more kilometres of tundra before reaching the drier slopes. To the east, the East Blackstone River must be crossed en route to higher places.

With those disclaimers in mind, the hiking here is wonderful. You can easily get off the beaten path in this part of the world, and the rewards will make the effort more than worthwhile.

The times given for the hikes in this section are based on average weather conditions and fitness levels. They are rough estimates at best. Use the information in this section as a general guide only (refer to hiking map, page 67).

Hike lengths and elevations are given in both metric and imperial measurements. The trailheads are identified only by kilometres because the road markers are placed every two kilometres (give or take a few) and labeled accordingly. The elevations given are only approximations.

MAPS

1:250,000 – Dawson (116 B & 116 C)

1:50,000 – Tombstone River (116 B/7), Upper Klondike River (116 B/8), North Fork Pass (116 B/9), Seela Pass (116 B/10)

DAY HIKES AND HIGHWAY POINTS OF INTEREST

Km 54 west	Twin Lakes Viewpoint Hike
Round trip:	16 km (10 miles)
Allow:	12 hours
Max. elevation:	1890 m (6200 feet)
Elevation gain:	1000 m (3300 feet)

This very long day hike takes you to a high viewpoint across the valley from two beautiful moraine lakes. The imposing grey walls of Mount Monolith tower above the aqua-blue lakes. Keep these hidden treasures in mind as you make your way through the forest at the start of this hike.

You can avoid the heavy bushwhacking along Wolf Creek by starting your hike at about Km 54 on the Dempster Highway. Just north of an access road leading to a microwave tower, there is a pulloff on the east side of the road.

Tony Gonda

Twin Lakes with Tombstone Mountain in the background.

Climb up a gentle, forested slope to the northwest for about 1.5 km (0.9 miles) until you can see Wolf Creek to the west and a narrow ridge to the northwest. Head for this ridge, crossing a tributary of Wolf Creek along the way. Follow the ridge, either on top of it or below the crest to Grizzly Pass, about 8 km (4.8 miles) from the highway. From Grizzly Pass, continue along the ridge to the northwest for 1 km (0.6 miles) until a view of Twin Lakes and Mount Monolith opens up. Return along the same route. Note that you are up high for much of this hike, and might want to take along extra water.

Km 58.5 west   Grizzly Valley Hike to Ridge Viewpoint

Round trip: 8 km (5 miles)
Allow: 2-4 hours
Max. elevation: 1600 m (5200 feet)
Elevation gain: 640 m (2100 feet)

This hike is very popular for several reasons. It is the fastest route into the Tombstone Range from the highway, and allows hikers to climb quickly above treeline where they are rewarded with spectacular views of the mountains, including Mount Monolith. Also, a trail has been worn in along the first few kilometres of this route, reinforcing its popularity.

The hike starts at a garbage dump where you can park your car, but do not camp here as the site often attracts bears. The future of this dump is uncertain, and there is some chance that it could be closed in the near future.

Topographic maps show incorrectly that the highway crosses Cairnes and Grizzly Creeks after they join. The dump is actually located between the two creeks, so no creek crossing is necessary as you travel up the ridge between Grizzly Creek and Cairnes Creek.

MICROWAVE TOWERS

A series of microwave towers were built along the Dempster Highway in the early 1990s. Placed about 30 kilometres apart, they provide a communications system for government employees who work along the road. The mobile radio system also serves Eagle Plains.

When the towers were built, concerns were raised that the access roads would increase hunting pressure on wildlife in the area. Although gates have been built across all of the roads, they are not always locked. While mountain bikers and hikers are welcome to use the roads, they are not intended for motorized access into the backcountry.

A cat trail starting at the far end of the dump eventually turns into a good footpath that leads you through the lower valley and onto the ridge. About an hour from the dump, a magnificent view of Mount Monolith opens up.

From here you can continue along the ridge for a ways, and then return by the same route. Watch closely to ensure that you pick up the trail again on the way down. It can be hard to find at times in the thickets of dwarf birch.

If you want to continue on to Grizzly Lake, avoid sidehilling on the slopes below for as long as possible by staying on the ridge until you reach a broad shoulder, about 4 kilometres along the ridge. From here pick your way downhill into Grizzly Valley and continue on to the lake.

As you climb out of the subalpine shrub birch, you might be able to spot a rare plant that grows in this area. *Phacelia mollis* has only been documented in seven locations in the Yukon. Please stay on the trail along the ridgeline to ensure that you do not trample this rare plant.

Km 61.5 west   Cairnes Ridge Viewpoint Hike

Round trip:	4 km (2.5 miles)
Allow:	4 hours
Max. elevation:	1700 m (5600 feet)
Elevation gain:	730 m (2400 feet)

Starting at Km 61.5, hike straight up the steep slope to the west. It is quite brushy down low, but about half way up you come to a gully that is relatively brush-free. Follow the gully to the top of the ridge where Mount Monolith suddenly comes into view to the west. Exceptional views of Mount Monolith and the North Klondike Valley make the climb well worthwhile.

If you want to continue ridge-walking, follow the crest 2 km (1.2 miles) to the northwest to Mount Cairnes. From there, you can travel northeast 1.5 km more (0.9 miles) along the ridge to Fold Mountain. At this point, the ridge starts a gradual descent back towards the highway at Km 66. This route is about 12 kilometres (7.2 miles) long.

Km 65 east   Klondike Highway Maintenance Camp

This is the first of three maintenance camps along the Yukon portion of the Dempster Highway. The staff at these camps do not provide visitor services, but they will assist travellers in true emergencies. Outrider Mountain forms a backdrop behind the compound.

Tony Gonda

Grizzly Lake is one of the most popular destinations in the region.

Km 65 west   Fold Mountain Hike

Round trip: 12 km (7.5 miles)
Allow: 9 hours
Max. elevation: 1970 m (6470 feet)
Elevation gain: 900 m (3000 feet)

The highpoints on this hike offer wonderful panoramas of the surrounding mountains. Start climbing where the ridge lies closest to the highway, directly across from the highway maintenance camp. Head west, picking a route through the least bushy areas until you reach a highpoint at 1680 m (5500 feet). Follow this ridge until it joins another ridge at 1890 m (6200 feet). The sweeping view here becomes even better if you travel another 3 kilometres (1.8 miles) southwest along the ridge to Fold Mountain. You can either retrace your steps for the return trip or descend to Fold Lake and hike out to Tombstone Campground. For more details on this return route, see the Fold Lake Hike description at Km 71.5.

Km 66 west   Rockslide

Old slide rubble looms over the highway here, south of the bridge that crosses the North Klondike River.

Km 66.5 east   Outrider Mountain

Round trip: 7 km (4.4 miles)
Allow: 5 hours
Max. elevation: 1600 m (5300 feet)
Elevation gain: 640 m (2100 feet)

From Outrider Mountain you can look down the North Klondike valley and into the smaller valleys to the east. Park just north of where the highway crosses the North

John Meikle

Rusty saxifrage

Klondike River. Head south, crossing the mouth of August 17 Creek. An old road that once made access through this section easier is now thickly overgrown, and you will have to tangle with some dense stands of willows along this route.

After crossing another intermittent stream, start heading for a rocky knoll on the skyline to the north of the peak. The rectangular object on the ridge is part of a microwave communications system that serves the highway. From the knoll, follow the curving ridge crest south to the peak. The more direct route, starting at Km 65, is not recommended. It involves a potentially dangerous river crossing as well as some bug-infested muskeg.

Km 67.5 east   Rock Glacier

A rock glacier descends from the peak to the northeast. These undulating tongues of rocks and boulders commonly begin as rockslides into steep cirques. If the rockfall continues, the rock glacier will creep its way down the slopes below. The toe of the glacier moves forward on a cushion of ground ice. Seen from above, the rock glacier has rolls of rubble on top of the lobe, and rocks at the front periodically topple forward into its path. Another rock glacier can be seen from the campground, descending from the peak to the southwest.

BUFFLEHEAD DUCKS

Buffleheads usually nest in tree cavities abandoned by flickers. These are found 1.5-6m (5-20 ft) high in a tree. When the chicks are 24 to 36 hours old, the mother repeatedly enters and leaves the nest cavity in order to entice the young to take the plunge. After the chicks fall to the ground, they must make the dangerous crossing to the relative safety of the water.

Km 70 west   Beaver Pond and Lodge

A family of beavers maintains a lodge and a series of terraced dams here when there is enough water. One spring, after a low snow year, the pond dried up. Those beavers did not survive, but another family eventually moved in after the pond waters were replenished. Bufflehead ducks and kestrels sometimes nest in the abandoned woodpecker holes found around the pond.

Km 71.5 west   Tombstone Campground and Dempster Interpretive Centre

The campground, located in the last stand of trees before the boreal forest gives way to the tundra, is a nice spot to relax for a day or two. A few of the campground's 36 sites are for tenting only. Firewood is available, and a screened-in cook shelter with a wood stove can make camping in bad weather more pleasant. Water is taken directly from the Klondike River at the back of the campground, and should be boiled before drinking.

Even if you do not plan to camp, visit the Dempster Interpretive Centre, located at the campground. The centre offers hands-on displays, a resource library, identification guides and much more. The naturalists who staff the centre offer guided nature walks and campfire talks. They can answer your questions about the land and the highway. A record of wildlife seen along the highway is kept here and all travelers are encouraged to add their sightings in the area.

CAMPGROUND ROUTES

Several walks of varying lengths start directly from the campground.

Self-guided nature walk

Allow: One-half hour

Interpretive signs along this loop trail describe interesting aspects of the area's natural history. Pick up the trail just north of the cook shelter.

River trail

Allow: One hour.

For a longer walk, continue north along a smaller trail at the point where the interpretive trail makes a sharp swing to the east. This trail, which parallels the North Klondike River, passes first through a tunnel of willows, and then through dwarf birch. After walking for about a kilometre, you will be able to see the braided gravel flats along the river, and sections of aufeis, or overflow ice.

Tombstone Mountain Viewpoint

One way:	2.5 km (1.5 miles)
Allow:	1.5 hours
Elevation gain:	150 m (500 feet)

If you want an even longer walk–and can arrange for someone to pick you up at the end – climb from the river trail to the viewpoint at Km 74. When you reach the section of trail where you can see the gravel flats along the river to your left, you will also see ahead of you the ridge that leads to the viewpoint. Make your way through the dark outcrops of rock on the slope, contouring northeast on higher ground to the viewpoint.

This walk could also be reversed, though you will want to ensure that you find the river trail after descending the slope from the viewpoint. If you aim for the area where the gravel flats start to constrict as the river flows down through the trees, you will intersect the trail close to the river.

Juri Peepre

Fold Lake is one of the many brilliantly colored tarns tucked into high basins in the Tombstone Range.

Fold Lake Hike

Round trip:	8 km (4.8 miles)
Allow:	6-8 hours
Max. elevation:	1500 m (5000 feet)
Elevation gain:	670 m (2200 feet)

This day trip ascends the slopes to the west of the campground, and continues on to several different alpine lakes. If the water levels are low enough, cross the river right behind the campground. If the water is too high to cross here comfortably, head upstream to where the river is more braided.

After passing through some poplar and spruce trees, aim for the right-hand side of the prominent rocky bowl directly behind the campground. You have to cross some spongy sections of tundra before you can begin climbing the drier slopes where travel is easier.

Continue climbing and heading west until you are above a steep north-facing gully. Continue contouring around the ridge above you, eventually descending a scree slope to two unnamed alpine lakes. Alpine plants such as purple saxifrage and prickly saxifrage grow in the numerous rock gardens. Shorebirds and waterfowl often use the lake, while caribou from the Hart River Herd sometimes graze on the grassy ledges.

If you decide to hike further to Fold Lake, continue west across a small stream and pass over the next ridge. There is less bushwhacking if you continue climbing so that you cross the ridge close to the peak. You can either return the same way you went up, or travel south high on the mountain before descending to the highway. See Fold Mountain Hike at Km 65 for more details on the southern route.

Charcoal Creek Ridge

Round trip:	7 km (4.4 miles)
Allow:	3-4 hours
Max. elevation:	1555 m (5100 feet)
Elevation gain:	550 m (1800 feet)

This hike ascends the ridge to the east of the campground. Follow the Charcoal Creek trail, which starts south of the interpretive centre, and cross the highway. Walk along the right side of the creek for a short ways, until the undergrowth makes it difficult to go any further. Look for one of two spots where indistinct trails head up the cutbank on your right.

Once you are on the slope, a more distinct trail leads up the face of the hillside to the crest of the ridge. After you have gained the ridge, you can ramble along it for hours, ascending Mt. Chester Henderson if you are feeling ambitious.

Juri Peepre

Aufeis, glaciated valleys and distant peaks can all be seen from the Tombstone Mountain Viewpoint.

This hike is not recommended during late July and early August when berries are ripe. Five types of berries grow in dense patches on the hillside, making it a popular feeding area for grizzly bears. The campground is closed when bears are feeding regularly in the area.

Km 74 west   Tombstone Mountain Viewpoint

The dramatic view from this pullout is one of the scenic highlights along the Dempster Highway. Tombstone Mountain, the prominent 2139 metre (7130 foot) peak for which the range is named, dominates the view, standing guard over the headwaters of the North Klondike River. Tombstone Mountain has always been a landmark for Yukon travellers. Prospectors during the Klondike Gold Rush called the mountain Tombstone because it resembled a grave-marker. Today its distinctive profile still guides pilots and hikers.

The mountains in this area are composed of syenite, a hard granitic rock formed when molten material intrudes older sedimentary layers. As the molten syenite squeezed upwards, it hardened into "pillar-like" structures called plutons. The spectacular forms of the Tombstones were exposed as the surrounding sedimentary rock eroded away.

During the last Ice Age, a valley glacier carved out this classic U-shaped valley. The ice stopped flowing near the big bend of the North Klondike River. As the glacier began to melt, retreating back up the valley, it dumped its load of rocks and gravel to form a terminal moraine. This feature has shaped the rolling landscape now seen in the valley bottom below you.

"The Surfbird is a Yukon specialty. These interesting birds winter on the rocky shores of the Pacific Ocean, but nest only in the Yukon and central Alaska. In summer, they seek out dry heath tundra on mountaintops for their nesting sites. If you are lucky enough to see this enigmatic species on its nesting grounds along the Dempster, stop for a moment to ponder the strange life of this chunky shorebird."

Pam Sinclair

Jennifer Staniforth

Km 74.5 east   Goldensides Mountain Hike

Round trip:	5 km (3 miles)
Allow:	3 hours
Max. elevation:	1830 m (6000 feet)
Elevation gain:	610 m (2000 feet)

Goldensides is the most popular day hike within range of the Tombstone Campground as the microwave tower road at Km 74.5 affords easy access to this pleasant peak. You can also start your hike directly from the campground.

By car, drive about halfway up the microwave tower road, and park where a chain blocks the road. By foot, follow the highway north about 0.5 km (0.3 miles) until you are just below the runaway truck ramp to the east. Climb the ridge, cross the runaway ramp and head straight for the mountain. Allow an extra hour for the round trip if you follow this route.

A fairly distinct trail leads from the radio tower to the loose shale beneath the peak. For the last 50 metres (165 feet) of the hike, choose your route carefully across the shale. The slope is steep here, and the shale can be very slippery when wet.

Surfbirds – a glorious sight – are sometimes seen on Goldensides. Watch for pikas and marmots in the boulder piles on the way up. Gentians and harebells are just some of the wildflowers growing along the route.

Km 77   Lil Creek Canyon/Aufeis

Lil Creek flows through a deep narrow canyon west of North Fork Pass, joining the North Klondike River just north of the campground. This crossing is an easy place to take a close look at aufeis or "overflow ice." In the spring, ice can completely choke the canyon, and massive chunks remain for most of the summer. Aufeis can also be seen on the braided section of the North Klondike River northwest of the campground.

Yukon Government/Catherine Kennedy

Sheets of aufeis can linger through the summer.

Aufeis forms during the extreme cold of winter, when there is relatively little snow cover to insulate the water. The water cannot percolate into the ground due to an impermeable mixture of permafrost and bedrock, so in shallow areas it starts to freeze solid. Upstream water flows over the new layer of ice, and continues to freeze in the shallow areas, creating a multi-layered ice sheet as winter progresses.

The flowing water also cuts channels in the ice, which show up at a variety of spots. In Lil Creek canyon, the ice sheet can be as thick as 4.5 metres (15 feet) due to the narrow constricted valley through which the creek flows.

If water levels are low enough, you can follow the creek downstream to the campground, but expect to get your feet wet. The 7 km (4.4 miles) hike takes about 3 hours. Follow the creek south 3.5 km (2.1 miles) to where it joins the braided section of the North Klondike River. Lil Creek joins the river from the north. Along the northeast bank of the river you can pick up the trail that leads back to the north end of the campground.

Km 78   Alpine tundra

The landscape begins to change dramatically as you travel out of the boreal forest into the wide-open world of the alpine tundra, the land above the trees. The word "tundra" comes from the Finnish word, "tunturi," meaning treeless plain. Wherever you see tundra, you can be pretty sure that the soil is permanently frozen below the surface. Only the thin, "active layer" of soil thaws during the summer. This top layer is not thick enough to support the roots of a tall tree, and only a few isolated trees straggle across the landscape.

The short growing season and desiccating winds force trees and other vegetation to grow low to the ground. In this land where trees fail, tiny wildflowers have evolved many successful adaptations and strategies. The stunted vegetation here might recall scenes from southern prairies and deserts, until the visitor takes a walk and discovers the rolling, hummocky and wet nature of tundra.

HART RIVER CARIBOU HERD

Scan the hillsides for caribou from the Hart River herd, as they are often seen on the tundra. The 1,200 animals in this herd of woodland caribou use North Fork Pass and the Blackstone Uplands as part of their summer range. Individuals or small groups may be spotted on windy slopes or snow patches where flies and mosquitoes are less of a bother. This is one of about 23 woodland caribou herds in the Yukon.

Km 78.2 east   Hart Pass Winter Road

One way to marshy section:	7 km (4.2 miles)
Allow:	2 hours
Max.elevation:	1370 m (4500 feet)
Elevation gain:	120 m (400 feet)

In the spring, this route can be very wet, but at drier times you can walk or mountain bike along portions of this deteriorating mining road. This track leads for 117 km (70 miles) to an abandoned lead/zinc mine located in the headwaters of the West Hart River. The road was built for winter use when the ground is frozen solid, so don't be fooled into thinking you can actually drive on it. The route runs over fairly flat terrain through a series of valleys. After about 7 kilometres (4.2 miles), it turns into a marshy quagmire, but it is a wonderful day hike to this point.

Caribou from the Hart River herd are often seen in this area. Sometimes wolves are sighted following in their hoofprints. Even if you don't see the animals, the muddy road provides an excellent surface for making casts of their tracks. Signs of wolf, caribou, moose or bear can almost always be found along the way.

The Hart Pass winter road is also a good route for a ski trip. You can follow the road back to the West Hart River and the old mine site. In the backcountry, be aware that you may be traveling on trappers' trails. Keep your dogs under control and out of their traps. Also, please respect their livelihood and don't tamper with traps or cabins.

Km 80   North Fork Pass Summit, McConnell Glacial Limit

At 1300 metres (4333 feet) above sea level, this continental divide is the highest point on the Dempster Highway. Except for the Eagle River and its tributaries, all waters north of this divide flow into the Beaufort Sea via the Mackenzie River system. Streams to the south are part of the Yukon River drainage that empties into the Bering Sea and the Pacific Ocean to the west.

The Dempster Highway follows the divide between the Yukon and Mackenzie River drainages for much of its length. During the last glacial advance, the Laurentide ice sheet blocked the normal easterly flow of the Bell and Porcupine Rivers. These rivers began to flow west and, even after the ice retreated, continued draining west toward the Yukon River drainage.

Towards the end of the last Ice Age, a glacier flowed out of the East Blackstone River valley and spread out into the North Fork Pass area. It retreated about 11,000 years ago, forming a terminal moraine as it dropped its load of rubble.

Further north the moraine has eroded away, but it can still be seen in this area. The hummocky landforms and U-shaped valley are classic glacial features. Continue on for 1 kilometre if you want to park and walk around this area.

Km 81 east	Angelcomb Peak/ Honeymoon Pit
One way to peak:	5 km (3 miles)
Allow:	2.5 hours
Max. elevation:	1920 m (6300 feet)
Elevation gain:	580 m (1900 feet)

This popular hike starts at what is probably the most well-known gravel pit on the Dempster Highway. It is dubbed Honeymoon Pit because Dave and Grace Mossop spent their honeymoon there in 1970. Mossop, a bird biologist who worked for the Yukon government for many years, set up ptarmigan survey plots in the area that same year. He returns every spring to do population counts of Willow Ptarmigan, Rock Ptarmigan and White-tailed Ptarmigan.

From the pit you can follow any of a number of game trails along the creek and up onto the gently sloping hill on the south side of the creek. In the interest of lessening impacts, try to pick the most well-defined trail that you see.

In summer, this hillside is blanketed with a wide variety of alpine flowers such as Ogilvie draba, violets, mountain heather and Lapland rosebay. The smell is heavenly if you get down on your knees. If you don't dawdle too long over the flowers, you can continue up through a saddle to the north and follow the ridge to the peak. From there you have a broad view north up the Blackstone valley as well as south back along the North Klondike and east into rarely traveled country. You can either descend the way you climbed up, or follow the ridges down to arrive at Km 84.5 on the highway.

Cameron Eckert

White-tailed Ptarmigan

PTARMIGANS AND GYRFALCONS

Ptarmigan have adapted very successfully to the harsh conditions of the north. In winter, their feathers turn white, camouflaging them from predators; their claws become significantly longer; and they develop dense feathers around their nostrils and on their feet. These feathers insulate their feet from the snow and act like snowshoes, reducing the depth the foot sinks into the snow by roughly 50 percent.

Ptarmigan are one of very few species to actually gain weight in the winter, and are an important food source for foxes, golden eagles and gyrfalcons. Three different species of ptarmigan – willow, rock and white-tailed – are found in this area.

The number of ptarmigan-breeding territories per square kilometre in the Ogilvie Mountains can range from a high of 90 at the peak of the ptarmigan cycle to a low of 25 when ptarmigan populations crash.

The breeding success of gyrfalcons closely follows the ten-year boom and bust cycle of the ptarmigan population. When ptarmigan numbers are at their peak, almost 50 percent of the adult gyrfalcons will breed. At the bottom of the cycle barely any of these raptors will breed successfully.

Look for the gyrfalcon nest on the cliff face to the west at Km 158 if you are traveling that far on the highway.

In the valley to the east you often see Dall sheep. A Golden Eagle's nest is perched on a ledge below the ridge you climb to reach the top. Orange lichen grows on the eagles' whitewash, marking their favourite perches. Golden Eagles are extremely sensitive to disturbance when breeding, so please do not approach the nest.

The grey towers and outcrops on this peak are composed of volcanic rock, formed when alkaline basalt erupted into undersea rifts 450 million years ago. If you hike up to the outcrops, look underneath overhangs for pillow lava. Gas bubbles in the molten lava created these rounded white shapes. Relics of volcanic glass can also be found, formed when lava came into contact with seawater.

Km 84 west   Permafrost Features

Seasonal frost mounds form on the gently sloping tundra beside this section of road every winter. The frost mounds occur where permafrost restricts the drainage of ground water. Eventually the build-up of water pressure between the frozen ground layer and the underlying permafrost causes the surface of the ground to form a dome. The mound usually collapses as the weather warms and the ice melts.

Earth hummocks, caused by frost action in fine-textured sediments, take a long time to form. Frost blisters, icing mounds and icing blisters also occur in the North Fork Pass area. The latter two are composed entirely of ice. For more information on permafrost features, refer to the Glossary of Landforms on page 15.

John Meikle

The slopes of Angelcomb Peak offer easy hiking for all ages.

Km 84.5   Angelcomb Peak Viewpoint

Km 88 west   Mount Adney Hike

Round trip: 8 km (4.8 miles)
Allow: 7 hours
Max. elevation: 1920 m (6300 feet)
Elevation gain: 760 m (2500 feet)

Mount Adney offers sweeping panoramic views in all directions. From the summit you can see Mount Auston, Blackstone Mountain, the East Blackstone valley and Foxy Creek to the northwest; Sheep Mountain and Angelcomb Peak to the northeast and east; and Rake Mountain to the north.

Park in the gravel pit at Km 88, and head for the southeast end of the nearest ridge. After leaving the highway, the first kilometre is flat and spongy tundra. Lurching across hummocks and tussocks can be a novel experience for a few metres, but after that the strain can start to wear on you. The next 3 kilometres (1.8 miles) is a climb to the summit. This hike is known to be a bit of a grunt, but the view from the top makes the effort worthwhile.

Km 88 west   Palsa Mounds

Just west of the gravel pit are three dome-shaped landforms called palsas. These frozen mounds, ranging in height from 1.5-4 metres, are usually found in areas of discontinuous permafrost. For more information see the Glossary of Landforms on page 15.

Km 90 east   Sheep Mountain Hike

Round trip:	4 km (2.4 miles)
Allow:	2.5 hours
Max. elevation:	1740 m (5700 feet)
Elevation gain:	580 m (1900 feet)

From Sheep Mountain you can see all the way north to Chapman Lake and the northern Ogilvies. To the south, you can see Mount Monolith and several high mountains near North Fork Pass. Start hiking where the highway is closest to the mountain. You will have to wade through several knee-deep channels of the East Blackstone River to reach its base.

On the south side of the mountain, head for the obvious saddle between a prominent knoll and a buttress higher on the same ridge. If you choose your route carefully, you should be able to avoid most of the brush past this point. At about 1740 m (5700 feet), a level ridge opens up and leads east for 5 kilometres (3 miles). Tread gently on the fragile ground cover and wildflowers you find here.

Yukon Government

Dall sheep can often be spotted on the rocky hillsides of both Angelcomb, shown here, and Sheep Mountain.

BLACKSTONE UPLANDS

The Blackstone Uplands stretch from North Fork Pass to Chapman Lake and beyond. They are drained by the Blackstone River, which is the size of a large creek at this crossing. This low-lying area is incredibly rich both biologically and culturally.

The plant communities are similar to ones found on the Yukon's North Slope, with extensive stretches of cottongrass and tussock tundra. Most of the archeological remains of prehistoric human communities have been found in this region, as well as the remains of turn of the century settlements such as Black City and Calico Town.

The Uplands teem with birdlife, and some people consider it to be the best area for birding along the Dempster Highway. Whimbrels and Upland Sandpipers are often seen nesting on the wet tundra. Northern Shrikes, Short-eared Owls, Long-tailed Jaegers and Golden Eagles fly overhead. In the breeding season, the air above the tundra is often filled with the distinctive sound of the Common Snipe.

The Blackstone Uplands form the cultural heartland of this region. Until the Dempster Highway was built, the traditional route into this country was up the Chandindu River valley, to the west of the Tombstone Range. Near the top of this drainage people would turn east and cross Seela Pass, and then follow Seela Creek and the Blackstone River into the heart of this region.

Shhhhh...Sheep

During May and June, Dall Sheep use the slopes on Sheep Mountain for lambing and nursery habitat. The crags offer safety from predators, and the south-facing slopes green up first in spring, providing food for the ewes.

It is strongly recommended that hikers stay away from this area when lambs are present. By the second week in June the sheep have usually retreated further back into the range, away from the highway. The 250 animals found here represent about one-quarter of the sheep population in the Dempster Highway area.

You may also see Golden Eagles soaring over the mountains or along cliff faces. Usually a pair of eagles nests in the vicinity, hunting the ground squirrels and marmots that live on the surrounding mountain slopes. They may also attack young lambs left unprotected by their mothers. Unlike Bald Eagles, which will feed on carrion, Golden Eagles prefer to kill their prey.

Km 90.5 east   Outfitter's Basecamp

In the Yukon, non-residents can only hunt with a licensed guide, and Pete Jensen is one of two guide-outfitters in the Tombstone area. You may see his horses grazing in the area before hunting season begins in August.

Yukon Government

The tundra of the Blackstone Uplands resembles landscapes found much further north.

Km 91 west   Foxy Creek

The valley to the west leads to a grassy plateau called Auston Pass. From there Arrow Creek flows down into the West Blackstone River. The dramatic summits of Mount Auston and Blackstone Mountain flank this valley to the north.

For a closer look at these summits, park in the pullout just north of the creek crossing and hike to the saddle low on the southeast ridge of Rake Mountain. Crossing this stretch of tundra should take about an hour. A horse trail starts on the other side of the saddle.

The Backcountry Travel Section (page 88) describes a route leading from the summits of the Cloudy Range out to the highway via Foxy Creek. The route could also be started from this end.

Km 92 west   Rake Mountain

Round trip:	6 km (3.7 miles)
Allow:	5 hours
Max. elevation:	1920 m (6300 feet)
Elevation gain:	760 m (2500 feet)

Rake Mountain offers a view very similar to that seen from Mount Adney (see km 87.5). The first 1.5 kilometres (0.9 miles) of the route crosses spongy tundra, also similar to Mount Adney. Do not be surprised if it takes you an hour to cover this distance. Ascend the ridge just north of the stream draining the east side of the peak. Mossy, moderate slopes lead to the summit. Rake Mountain also provides the easiest access to the summits of Mount Auston and Blackstone Mountain to the west.

Km 96.7   Ice-Wedge Polygons

The tundra along both sides of the road in this area was disturbed when the road right-of-way was reconstructed in 1984. Excavation in the area exposed a large network of ice-wedge polygons. Ice wedges, which form in the upper portion of the permafrost, began melting when the groundcover was disturbed. Look for actively melting ice wedges further back from the edge of the road.

John Meikle

Rocky outcrops called tors show where weathering, not glaciation, has shaped the landscape.

NORTHERN ROAD CONSTRUCTION PROBLEMS

Road construction is a challenge in permafrost areas, and many lessons were learned while building the Dempster Highway. In 1961, roads were built on permafrost by scraping off the surface, and then laying down a thick layer of gravel. Unfortunately, the gravel pad for this section of road was delayed for a year, and the exposed permafrost melted, creating shallow thermokarst ponds. A new alignment had to be made.

For the remainder of the highway a thick gravel pad was laid over undisturbed vegetation to minimize temperature fluctuations. Trenches were dug uphill from the highway to channel water seepage in the active layer of the soils. Another recent technique used in permafrost areas involves laying an insulation or moisture barrier in the roadbed.

Km 98 west   Road Access: microwave towers

The access road to the west leads to a microwave tower, one in a series along the Dempster Highway. If you continue up the ridges above the microwave tower, eventually you will see a mining exploration road zig-zagging up a hillside to the west.

The road was used to explore claims that lapsed in 1991. Exploration work was done on these claims in the mid-1980s, but the scars are still clear more than a decade later.

Km 102.5   Two Moose Lake

It is worth planning a stop at the interpretive viewing area here. The twilight hours of summer are a favourite feeding time for moose, and they can often be seen browsing on willows or even diving for pondweed, a preferred food. Moose are not abundant in the Blackstone Uplands, but they make up for their low numbers in size. The Alaska Yukon or tundra moose (*Alces alces gigas*) is the largest subspecies of moose in North America.

About 30 species of waterbirds use this area. From the wildlife-viewing platform here you can look for Northern Pintails, Scaup, Oldsquaws, Northern Shovellers and Horned Grebes. Occasionally a swan will visit. You might also see Red-necked Phalaropes spinning like tops around the margins of the lake while they feed. This bizarre-looking behaviour is thought to stir up food lodged on the bottom. The sandpiper-like Phalaropes have lobed toes that make them equally at home wading or swimming.

Km 105   Moraines

Moraines border the road for the next nine to 10 kilometres, showing where glaciers dumped their loads of debris as they melted. One of the last signs of glaciation is the terminal moraine along the Blackstone River. It marks where a small glacier flowing out of the valley to the west dropped its load of rubble before it started to retreat. This glacier received so little snow that it only spread a short distance north and south into the main valley of North Fork pass. This region has probably been free of glaciers for about 10,000 years.

As you continue north, you enter the glacial refugium of Beringia. Notice how the profiles of the mountains change in this region. Weathering replaces glaciation as the main force shaping the mountains, so you will no longer see the moraines and glacial-carved cirques typical of the Southern Ogilvies. Wearing mountains down by weathering requires an exceedingly long period of time. Water, wind, and temperature changes break the rock apart.

In the Northern Ogilvies, tors often crown the ridge tops. These castle-like masses of rock, typical features of unglaciated areas, have not yet succumbed to weathering.

Km 107.5 east   Fishing

If you have a fishing licence, consider parking at the pullout and trying your luck along this braided section of the Blackstone River. Arctic grayling can be found in eddies formed by the braids. You can also sometimes catch char in the Blackstone River. Another good spot for fishing is at Km 117.

Km 114.8   West Blackstone Crossing

The west and east forks of the Blackstone River join just to the east of this crossing. The Gwich'in name for the Blackstone, Tth'oh zraii njik, means "black boulder creek," a reference to the black shale in this area. Scores of cliff swallows build their mud nests beneath the highway bridge. A Red-throated Loon often nests in the ox-bow lake near the bridge.

Watch for Arctic Terns skimming or hovering over the water. The terns nest on gravel bars in the braided channels of the river. Arctic Terns are among the long-distance champions of the bird world. They migrate nearly 20,000 kilometres from the north to Antarctic regions, reaching it just in time for another summer. These birds experience more hours of daylight than any other species on earth.

Km 115   Pingos

Once you have crossed the river and gained a bit of elevation, look upriver about 5 kilometres (3.1 miles). The two rounded mounds rising from the valley floor to the west are pingos. These unique permafrost features have cores of solid ice, and continue growing as long as there is a source of water that allows the ice core to expand. These two pingos are thought to be more than 5,000 years old. There is some debate over whether these landforms are open-system pingos, formed by moving groundwater, or closed-system pingos which form on flat poorly drained terrain. For more information on pingos see the Glossary of Landforms on page 15.

Km 116 west   Chapman Lake

This 3-kilometre long lake, the largest of the many lakes and ponds that dot the Blackstone Uplands, was named for Ernest Chapman, a local trader, trapper and prospector. The complex array of sandy ridges and ponds around the lake was formed by a moraine in which several large blocks of ice melted, leaving hollows.

The Gwich'in have a much more descriptive name for this lake. Ets'ik Goghwar means "twisted guts" as the Gwich'in reported that the entrails of the fish caught there were often tangled.

Chapman Lake was at the end of the road in 1964 when the Canadian government dropped the highway project for other priorities. Work continued on a smaller scale, and the road was officially opened in 1979.

BLACK CITY

Traces of 18 different dwellings have been found at a site in this area. The oldest dwellings, which are probably a century old, were round houses dug down into the ground. Usually used in winter, they were covered with caribou skin. Remains of tent sites from the 1910s have also been found, as well as the remains of tent houses built on log bases.

Several of the older houses contained a chee, a flat rock for pounding dry caribou meat for making ettsu, which combined meat, grease and dried berries.

The Gwich'in caught grayling in the Blackstone River and dried them for use during the long winter. They hunted caribou as they crossed between the Blackstone and Hart Rivers. During the Klondike Gold Rush, Gwich'in hunters sold meat in Dawson City. Black City was an important stopping point for these market hunters.

Resources such as firewood were limited so families spread out, camping together in small groups. Little sign of the encampments remains except for old axe-cut trees in the groves east of the road.

A Tukudh Gwich'in man named Jarvis Mitchell operated a trading post for a short time at a site called Calico Town near Chapman Lake. It opened in about 1900, but closed soon afterwards, and some of the cabins were never completed. It was called Calico Town because Gwich'in women would change into their fancy calico dresses there before heading into Dawson City.

Northern Crossroads

This region was familiar to early travellers long before the days of highways and aircraft. It was a winter crossroads for Han and Gwich'in peoples from the Old Crow, Dawson and Fort McPherson areas. Later the Northwest Mounted Police passed through the area on their winter patrols between Dawson, Fort McPherson and Herschel Island.

In some years animals from the Porcupine Caribou Herd use this area as an early winter range. Usually in October the caribou migrate across the tundra between Chapman Lake and Cache Creek at Km 128. After rutting on the open shrubby tundra, the herd moves on to winter areas along the Hart River.

Km 117.5 east	Mount Vines/Pilot's Peak Hike
Round trip:	8 km (5 miles)
Allow:	5 hours
Max. elevation:	1680 m (5500 feet)
Elevation gain:	700 m (2300 feet)

On the ridge to the east, you can see where valley glaciers once ground the slopes smooth. Above the level of the ice, blocks of sedimentary rock were left untouched. Park in the gravel pit at Km 117.5 and cross the nearby Blackstone River where it is wide and braided. In spring, or after a heavy rain, this crossing can be dangerous. Continue across a short stretch of tundra to the trees at the base of the mountain. As you reach the upper end of the trees, leave the creekbed to your left and climb straight up the mountainside. Don't be daunted by the looming cliffs above. There are many routes through them.

Juri Peepre

Alpine ridges in the Cloudy Range invite exploration.

CANOEING THE BLACKSTONE

The Blackstone River parallels the Dempster Highway for about 60 kilometres, but further north, at about Km 140, the highway jogs left and the river heads off into wild country. The Blackstone flows for about 135 kilometres through roadless terrain before joining the Ogilvie River to the north.

The unglaciated mountains along this stretch of river offer many opportunities for hiking right from the water's edge. The birdwatching along the Blackstone is also excellent. But, to be brief, this is not classic canoe country. The rapids are no harder than Class II, but there are numerous tight corners and lots of sweepers. Kayaks can be a better choice for this shallow, braided stream, especially in low water.

When the Blackstone empties into the Ogilvie River, paddlers face a tough choice. They can line their boats up the Ogilvie for 40 kilometres back to the highway, or they can continue downstream to the Peel, and paddle more than 400 kilometres to Fort McPherson, NWT. The Peel option also involves a 8-10 kilometre portage around the violent whitewater in Aberdeen Canyon.

In many areas of the Tombstones, you are bound to experience the fine art of bush-whacking, also known as willow-bashing. People can react very differently to this total immersion in the world of shrubs. Some take it as a challenge, while others remember the high country that is their goal and just endure the grasping branches the best that they can.

Keep in mind that traversing above the level of the shrubs is often worthwhile, even if it means climbing higher than your final destination requires. Battling the brush can demand more energy than gaining extra elevation.

If you end up in the shrubs, some route-finding connoisseurs recommend aiming for any trees visible in a brushy section, claiming that you are more likely to pick up animal trails by travelling from tree to tree. And if the animals have perversely picked a different strategy, the trees always provide a good resting spot.

BACKCOUNTRY TRAVEL IN THE TOMBSTONES/BLACKSTONE UPLANDS

Even in the Yukon, home to Canada's highest peaks and many dramatic mountain ranges, the Tombstone Range stands out. From the highway, glimpses of Tombstone Mountain show why this peak is arguably the most distinctive mountain in the territory. You must hike into the Tombstones to appreciate Mount Monolith and the other granitic peaks of this range.

The Tombstone Range is less than 20 kilometres long as the crow flies, but a lot of vertical relief is packed into this compact size. Tombstone Mountain and Mount Monolith rise nearly 1000 metres from the valley floor below them. Many faces rear 600 metres and more from high scree slopes.

Most backpackers head into the heart of the Tombstones, overlooking the potential of other wonderful areas. In the Cloudy, Blackstone and Seela Ranges, there is still room for exploration. You could wander for weeks on the high ridges of these valleys without seeing a soul. Most of the potential routes through these ranges have not yet been documented.

In the following guide, the most detailed information is given for the three main routes into the Tombstones. **Please remember that even these routes do not follow established trails**. Only at the start of the Grizzly Valley hike has repeated use worn in a trail. People must often rely on their own route-finding abilities, and the thick brush encountered in some areas can defeat even experienced hikers. Use the information in this section as a general guide only.

These routes are described in stages, and include day hike options along the way. Grizzly Creek Valley, Wolf Creek Valley and the North Klondike River Valley routes all allow relatively quick access to the Tombstone Range from the Dempster Highway. The old Dawson fire access road, the fourth route, follows part of the historic system of ditches and flumes that supplied water

---

Dave Mossop

Many Golden Eagles nest in the Tombstone region.

and power to the Klondike gold fields. This long, swampy route is seldom used, except in winter, so it is not described in this guide. For a brief description of it see Walter Lanz's book *Along the Dempster Highway.*

Some of the exploration possibilities for the Cloudy Range are also described. These weathered sedimentary mountains are more subdued than the Tombstones, their rugged neighbours to the south. But the endless waves of ridges in this area are also appealing, and offer many intriguing possibilities for routes.

Keep in mind that the existing topographical maps cannot be completely trusted. Some of the mapping mistakes have been noted in the route descriptions, but there might be others. Also be aware that the tundra can distort your sense of distance. Without trees for reference, a fairly long distance may appear quite short. Walking on the deceptively flat tundra can also take a lot more time than anticipated due to hummocks, tussocks and soft ground. The times given for the hikes in this section are based on average weather conditions and fitness levels. They are rough estimates at best.

Finally, please remember bear encounters are always a possibility in the Tombstone Range and Blackstone Uplands area. Read the bear aware section and take all the suggested precautions. Staff at the Dempster Interpretive Centre can give you information on bear sightings in the area.

Route No. 1: Wolf Creek Valley

This valley offers several routes into the heart of the Tombstones, but none of them is particularly easy because of the brush and forest at lower elevations. If you are keen to do a circle route on the south side of the Tombstone Range, consider hiking up Grizzly Valley, crossing Grizzly Pass, and descending the ridge north of Wolf Creek to Km 54 on the highway. It is much easier to head downhill through trees and brush than to climb up through them.

There are two routes between the highway, and the confluence of Wolf Creek and Twin Lakes Creek.

Twin Lakes via Wolf Creek Valley

Trailhead:	Km 50.7
One way:	7 km (4.3 miles)
Allow:	10 hours
Elevation gain:	250 m (830 feet)
Elevation loss:	210 m (700 feet)

This route is not popular because of the dense bushwhacking at the start. The bushes are mainly above head height and the mosquitoes in the valley bottom are reputed to be fierce. People have come back with stories about walking in the creek for most of the distance to avoid the bushes. It is also difficult to find a spot to camp in the valley bottom below treeline.

Twin Lakes via Grizzly Pass

Trailhead:	Km 54
One way:	12 km (7.5 miles)
Allow:	9 hours
Elevation gain:	1,130 m (3700 feet)
Elevation loss:	850 m (2800 feet)

The Twin Lakes Viewpoint Hike, described in the day hikes section on page 70, takes you as far as a ridge east of Twin Lakes. If your final destination is Twin Lakes, descending from this high point is too difficult unless you are blessed with the agility of a mountain goat. Instead, once you are on the northwest-trending ridge headed towards Grizzly Pass, begin contouring around the ridge to the west and descend into the Twin Lakes drainage. Around the lakes you will see stunning moss and rock gardens surrounding small waterfalls. Shorebirds and waterfowl also use the lakes. It is a beautiful spot to camp.

Tombstone Brink Round Trip Hike
from confluence of Wolf Creek and Twin Lakes Creek

Round trip:	12 km (7.5 miles)
Allow:	8 hours
Max. elevation:	1740 m (5700 feet)
Elevation gain:	670 m (2200 feet)

This side trip takes you into the very heart of the Tombstone Range, and rewards hikers with stunning views of the most prominent peaks in this area. It also allows non-climbers to experience the airy heights of this range. From its confluence with Wolf Creek, follow Twin Lakes Creek north one kilometre (0.6 miles) until you see a hanging valley to the west. Travel up this valley past two beautiful alpine lakes. The final 2 kilometres (1.2 miles) past the lakes to the crest of the ridge ends in a steep 100 m (330 foot) climb. Be careful as you approach the ridge crest as there is a sheer drop on the north side. From the top, there are stunning views of Tombstone Mountain to the west and Mount Monolith to the northeast.

Pat Morrow

North Face of Mount Monolith

Wolf Pass
from confluence of Wolf Creek and Twin Lakes Creek to Spotted Fawn Gulch

One way: 11 km (7 miles)
Allow: 8 hours
Max. elevation: 670 m (2200 feet)
Elevation loss: 520 m (1700 feet)

Follow Wolf Creek west. The brush is not nearly so thick through this section of Wolf Creek as it is lower down. Numerous game trails also help ease the way. After 7 kilometres (4.3 miles) you reach a seemingly impassable ridge which stretches north from the western end of the valley. Near its southern edge is a rocky slope which non-climbers can manage. The pass is at an elevation of 1740 m (5700 feet).

On the west side of the pass, a pair of brilliant blue lakes mark the Little Twelve Mile River drainage. Follow the sparsely vegetated northern slopes of the valley for 3 kilometres (1.9 miles) west. Then descend to the mouth of Spotted Fawn Gulch below Tombstone Mountain.

CLIMBING IN THE TOMBSTONE RANGE

Some climbers refer to the rock found in the Tombstone Range as "granola bar granite." Isolated patches of good rock can be found on some walls, but you have to choose your routes carefully.

The 5.8 km route on Mount Monolith was not climbed until 1978. Some parties have taken advantage of the midnight sun and reached the summit of this long route during the middle of the night.

The Candlestick, northwest of Mount Monolith, has also been climbed a number of times. This spire of rock has a blocky split summit. Some climbers scale the face. Others have climbed up the backside and only encountered technical sections close to the summit. There are also routes on the north face of Tombstone Mountain. Other smaller peaks have provided good climbing and have been nicknamed in keeping with the "tombstone" funereal theme. For more information and specific routes you can find articles in back issues of the Canadian Alpine Journal. Some of the first ascents are documented in Vol. 61, 1978 and Vol. 62, 1979.

Panorama Peak Round Trip Hike
from Spotted Fawn Gulch

Round Trip: 8 km (5 miles)
Allow: 4 hours
Max. elevation: 2100 m (6900 feet)
Elevation gain: 880 m (2900 feet)

To reach Panorama Peak, follow the crest of the ridge 4 kilometres (2.4 miles) directly northeast from Spotted Fawn Gulch. Peaks melt away into the distance in all directions, creating a truly stunning sight.

Tombstone Mountain Round Trip Hike
from Spotted Fawn Gulch

Round trip: 11 km (7 miles)
Allow: 7 hours
Max. elevation: 2192 m (7191 feet)
Elevation gain: 1000 m (3300 feet)

This route up the backside of Tombstone Mountain allows confident alpine hikers to ascend high up the mountain. Hike north along the gently rising ridge on the west side of Spotted Fawn Gulch. About 4 kilometres (2.4 miles) from the gulch, the views start to open up. Keep following the gentle rise and fall of the ridge until you reach "the tombstone" at its northern end. The final 150 metres (500 feet) become progressively more challenging.

The last 20-30 metres of the route is very steep and exposed, and a rope would be needed to climb it safely. Remember that you are in a very remote area, and turn back well before you reach the limits of your abilities.

Spotted Fawn Gulch to Little Twelve Mile Flume Intake

One way: 7 km (4.4 miles)
Allow: 4 hours
Elevation loss: 270 m (900 feet)

Follow the Little Twelve Mile River 7 kilometres (4.3 miles) west from Spotted Fawn Gulch. The flume intake, a broken dam, lies among the first trees below treeline.

Yukon Government/John Meikle

The Little Twelve Mile Power Plant was once the site of a thriving community.

Check the gravel bars along the Little Twelve Mile and Chandindu Rivers for attractive white crystals called pseudoleucite, which can be as big as golf balls at times. Pseudoleucite is derived from a dark-grey rock called tinguaite, which is known for its high fluoride content and radioactivity.

Tinguaite forms the intermediate ring of the three concentric phases of rock that form the pluton centred on Tombstone Mountain. Identified by its distinctive "egg-carton" surface, tinguaite is abundant around the head of Spotted Fawn Gulch, where it forms outcrops more than 1000 metres wide.

In the 1920s, this area was mined for silver-bearing galena, the shiny blue-grey ore of lead. Mule-trains hauled eight tonnes of ore out of this valley, but little evidence of this venture remains on the surface today.

Flume to the Goldfields

The Little Twelve Mile Flume Intake was one of two intake points for a massive water diversion project that led all the way to the goldfields by Bonanza Creek. The Yukon Ditch has been called an engineering feat comparable to the building of the Panama Canal, and some engineers did work on both of these projects.

The water was siphoned from both the Little Twelve Mile River and the Tombstone River, and transported about 112 kilometres (70 miles) to Bonanza Creek. A combination of wooden flumes resting on trestles and ditches dug into the earth maintained the necessary grade. Pumps were not necessary as the system relied totally on gravity.

When water had to be moved from one valley to the next, gravity and water volume were used to push the water up the hillside. This required a tremendous build-up of water pressure, so metal pipe, imported from Pittsburgh and Germany, was used in these sections. Tongue and groove redwood, imported from California, was used in areas where the water pressure was lower. The flumes were made of local spruce.

The water (55,000 gallons per minute at Bonanza Creek) was used in hydraulic operations to separate the gold from the gravel. The Little Twelve Mile Power Plant produced 1200 kilowatts of power, which was used to run the massive dredges in the goldfields. The whole project cost $3 million to build in 1906 and paid for itself many times over before it was shut down in 1933. For more information on the Yukon Ditch, see page 43.

Little Twelve Mile Flume Intake to Power Plant

One way:	8 km (5 miles)
Allow:	7 hours
Elevation loss:	240 m (800 feet)

Either continue along the Little Twelve Mile River or follow the dilapidated flume. The river route is bushy. The flume route follows the river to the south. All that is left of the flumes are piles of rotted boards embedded with thousands of rusty nails. Unless you are a history buff, the river route is the better bet. If you are not a history buff, consider turning around and exploring the high country. The scenery is much more exciting and you can also spot (and avoid) bears much more easily.

If you are interested in the historic sites, watch for the camp of eight or nine buildings at Dinner Gulch, labelled as Flume Creek on topographic maps, on the Little Twelve Mile River. Some of the cabins still have intact roofs. Please leave any artifacts you may find for the next traveller to enjoy.

Sheep Mountain Pass: Little Twelve Mile Flume Intake to Tombstone Flume Intake

One way:	8 km (5 miles)
Allow:	6 hours
Elevation gain and loss:	530 m (1800 feet)

Sheep Mountain Pass is the most common route used to traverse between the Little Twelve Mile River and the Tombstone River, but be aware that Tombstone Valley west of the peak offers a high risk of close-up bear encounters.

From the Little Twelve Mile flume intake, continue down the river about 0.5 kilometres (0.3 miles). Then climb the steep, but passable, slopes to the north. The pass, located at an elevation of 1500 m (4900 feet) is about 2 kilometres (1.2 miles) west of Sheep Mountain. Traverse the flanks of the mountain and its sister peak for about 2.5 kilometres (1.5 miles) as you travel north. Descend moderate slopes into the Tombstone River valley to meet the flume intake. The dry south-facing slope is described as fairly easy, though there is lots of bushwhacking up to 1400 metres (4300 feet).

Parties have also reported crossing the Tombstone Range further east, between Sheep Mountain and Tombstone Mountain. But only very experienced hikers confident on steep, exposed, rocky terrain should consider exploring these routes; a mountaineering background is advised.

One of the alternate routes heads south up Diabase Creek, which is just east of the flume intake. Diabase, a distant relative of granite, is a charcoal grey-rock that forms when magma cools slowly at great depths.

From a small lake at the head of Diabase Creek, head almost due east to a slightly larger lake. This lake is located about 3 kilometres (1.9 miles) northwest of the confluence of Spotted Fawn Gulch and the Little Twelve Mile River.

The north-facing slope is described as rocky, but not too loose. The south-facing slope is a slippery scree slope that drops off precipitously for a long ways. One person describes it as being not for the faint-hearted.

At least one party has also descended into the Tombstone drainage just west of Tombstone Mountain, but again, these are not recommended routes. They've been done, but they are not for everyone. If you get into trouble, you are a long ways from help.

Route No. 2: Grizzly Creek Valley

Dempster Highway to Grizzly Lake

Trailhead:	Km 58.5
One way:	9 km (5.6 miles)
Allow:	9 hours
Elevation gain:	700 m (2300 feet)
Elevation loss:	240 m (800 feet)

Expect to see other cars at this trailhead as Grizzly Valley is the most well traveled backcountry route in the Tombstones. For the first several kilometres a worn-in trail makes the hiking easy by Tombstone standards, and you climb above the treeline fairly quickly. For complete information on the first 4 kilometres (2.5 miles) of the trail, read the Grizzly Valley Hike information for Km 58.5 in the day hike section.

Once you reach the ridge and are faced by the first of a series of rocky knolls, it can be very tempting to start contouring down into the inviting green of the valley below, particularly when carrying a heavy pack. Resist the temptation and stay on the ridge. If you descend, you will have to contend with heavy brush lower down, and side-hill for long stretches across scree and boulders.

A path worn in by hikers who also have chosen the higher route continues for a ways along the ridge. Continue northwest until you cross above an intermittent stream and reach a broad shoulder on the ridge. From here begin picking your way down towards the creek.

Keep in mind that this route can be treacherous when wet. The black foliose lichen growing on the rocks makes them particularly slippery when wet. Look for hoary marmots and pikas among the rocks.

There is good camping near Grizzly Lake, which is at an elevation of 1370 m (4500 feet). But please choose your campsite with wildlife in mind. Avoid camping next to the lake as Buffleheads and other puddle ducks like to nest along the shoreline.

Also, animals in this watershed regularly cross both Glissade and Grizzly Passes, so please do not inhibit their movements by camping at the bases of these passes. One possible campsite is on a forb meadow about 250 - 350 metres SE of the lake on a bench above the wet valley floor. There is also a lovely camping spot at a small lake south of Grizzly Lake.

Grizzly Lake lies on the south side of the Tombstone Range.

Grizzly Lake could already be contaminated with Giardia, so either boil your water or use a water filter here. Please be careful to leave no trace of your passage. If you do see signs of other campers, please clean them up for the benefit of both yourself and others.

Phacelia mollis, a rare plant (fewer than 7 documented locations in Yukon according to the territorial conservation data) grows adjacent to the existing Grizzly Lake trail just as one gets out of the subalpine shrub birch and continues along the ridgeline en route to Grizzly Lake. To avoid trampling this rare plant, please stay on the existing trail along the ridge.

Perilous Pass Round Trip Hike
from Grizzly Lake

Round trip:	4 km (2.5 miles)
Allow:	4 hours
Elevation gain:	1770 m (5800 feet)
Elevation loss:	400 m (1300 feet)

Hike along the north side of Grizzly Lake until you reach a small stream that flows in from the northwest. Follow the stream to the head of a small valley. From this point, head north towards a steep slope that leads to a pass. Climb 100 metres (330 feet) up this boulder-strewn route to reach the narrow pass, just below the towering walls of Mount Monolith. This hike takes you within 400 metres (1300 feet) of the summit of the peak without any technical climbing.

Grizzly Pass
Grizzly Lake to confluence of Wolf Creek and Twin Lakes Creek

One way: 5 km (3 miles)
Allow: 3.5 hours
Elevation gain: 370 m (1200 feet)
Elevation loss: 670 m (2200 feet)

You cross Grizzly Pass when traversing between Grizzly Creek and Wolf Creek to the south. From the southeast corner of Grizzly Lake, follow the steep stream that flows from the heights to the south. When you reach a small pond at the headwaters of the stream, continue up a rocky ridge to Grizzly Pass at an elevation of 1740 metres (5700 feet). From here follow a gentle slope down for 3 kilometres (1.8 miles) to the confluence of Twin Lakes Creek and Wolf Creek.

Glissade Pass
Grizzly Lake to Divide Lake

One way: 6.5 km (4 miles)
Allow: 4 hours
Elevation gain: 425 m (1400 feet)
Elevation loss: 425 m (1400 feet)

The route from Grizzly Lake to the North Klondike valley and Divide Lake crosses Glissade Pass. From the east end of Grizzly Lake, take the first slope to the north.

Crossing the pass from south to north is easiest as the vegetation covering the south side makes the steep climb relatively easy. The pass is at an elevation of 1800 metres (5900 feet).

Descending the scree-covered north side can be tricky if it is wet or snowy. "Boot skiing" works well on this type of scree slope, as each step can carry you down several metres. When snow still covers the pass, consider crossing later in the day when the snow might be softer and you can "plunge-step" down it more easily.

As you descend the north side of the pass, it can be tempting to contour around to Divide Lake by staying up on the bench west of the creek below the pass. This bench offers a good campsite, but unfortunately it tapers off into steep faces and cliffs above the North Klondike River valley. Stay low in the valley, and pick a route once you can contour around the ridge between the two drainages.

Al Aasman

Descending the north side of Glissade Pass.

When you reach the North Klondike River, follow it southwest to its headwaters at Divide Lake.

Route No. 3: Upper North Klondike River Valley

Dempster Highway to Divide Lake

Trailhead: Km 71.5
One way: 16 km (10 miles)
Allow: 10 hours
Elevation gain: 340 m (1100 ft)
Max. elevation: 1370 m (4500 ft)

Even though this route is infamous for its thick brush, it is still travelled regularly. Reaching scenic Divide Lake, the source of the North Klondike River, is ample reward for the effort. The willow-bashing will soon be forgotten if you proceed on to Tombstone Pass and the upper Tombstone Valley. The alpine area between Mount Monolith and Tombstone Mountain is one of the scenic highlights of the entire range.

From the north end of the Tombstone Campground, follow the trail along the east side of the North Klondike River. The braided, shallow section of river about 2 kilometres (1.2 miles) from the campground is a good place to cross.

After crossing, you have two route options traversing the south side of the valley above the level of the shrubs or following a horse trail along the valley bottom. The horse trail continues for about 7 kilometres up the valley. If you miss the horse trail, and really want to stay low, look for the numerous game trails that parallel the river. They tend to stop and start, but can often be linked together for easier passage. When you do have to resort to bashing through the brush, remember to be bear aware and make noise to announce your presence.

The preferred route is along the south side of the valley. If you climb to about 1370 metres (4500 ft) you can traverse above the shrubs in the valley. This higher route also allows you to camp in and explore spectacular side valleys carved out of sedimentary rock. Steep walls and castellated cliffs form backdrops for the small lakes found in these drainages, and the surrounding tundra is covered with wildflowers at the peak of summer.

In the main valley, there are very few dry camping spots before Divide Lake. Please try to pick the most durable ground possible when camping at Divide Lake.

John Meikle

Candle ice can linger on Talus Lake into June.

Divide Lake to Talus Lake via Tombstone Pass

One way: 10 km (6 miles)
Allow: 3 hours
Elevation gain
and loss: 150 m (500 feet)

Hiking through this area is one of the highlights of the Tombstone Range. Ahead of you, Tombstone Mountain shoots up almost 1000m (3300 ft) from the valley floor. The sedimentary peaks of the Cloudy Range form a rampart to the northwest, while the knife-edge ridges and crests of the Tombstones line the southeast side of the valley.

From Divide Lake, head southwest over Tombstone Pass to Talus Lake, located at an elevation of 1530 metres (5000 ft). The pass lies only 2 kilometres (1.2 miles) west of Divide Lake, the headwaters of the North Klondike River. The open sweeps of tundra covering this low easy pass contrast sharply with the towering peaks and massive rock walls of the surrounding Tombstone massif.

Allow plenty of times for exploring this area as the small cirque lakes, or tarns, tucked into several of the side valleys are the hidden jewels of this landscape. Their aqua-blue waters are set off dramatically by the steep rock walls that surround them. The hike from the pass to the base of Tombstone Mountain is an easy stroll compared with most of the hiking in the Tombstone area. Only a few rocky spots and some soggy tundra below the west-facing cirque basins will slow your progress.

Please avoid walking across a fragile area of patterned ground west of Divide Lake. The sorted circles of rock there are a distinctive frost feature that should be preserved.

Talus Lake, 4 km (2.4 miles) west of the pass, is not a desirable place to camp. For one, vegetation at the south end of the lake has been damaged. The rocks covering most of the area also make camping less than comfortable. Consider camping further north towards Tombstone Pass, or at a tarn in one of the side valleys.

Pat Morrow

Tombstone Pass

Talus Lake to Tombstone Flume Intake

One way: 11 km (7 miles)
Allow: 6 hours
Elevation of
flume intake: 975 m (3200 feet)
Elevation loss: 400 m (1300 feet)

Be prepared for tall brush as you follow the Tombstone River west past Talus Lake. If you're lucky, you may chance upon an obscure horse trail that follows the north side of the Tombstone River. But even on the trail, the going is still tough.

You have the familiar Tombstone choice here of side-hilling across rocky slopes if you don't like bushwhacking. The north-facing slope is better for traversing.

This hiking route is not recommended in August when berries are ripe. Large patches of blueberries located a few kilometres past the lake attract bears to the area. Bear rubbings on the trees are positive proof of these visits. If you do decide to travel this route during berry season, be very careful.

Good camping can be found a short ways up the creek that flows south into the Tombstone River across from the flume intake. The intake lies below treeline.

The Tombstone flume intake is the second of the two intakes that channeled water to the goldfields at Bonanza Creek. For more information on the project, see the "Flume to the Goldfields" description on page 92.

Tombstone Flume Intake to Twelve Mile Power Plant

One way:	13 km (8 miles)
Allow:	12 hours
Elevation loss:	270 m (900 feet)
Final elevation:	700 m (2300 feet)

The many negatives outweigh the few positives on this route. Unless you have an overwhelming interest in the historical sites in this part of the backcountry, stay in the high country. This route goes through heavy, miserable brush, so be prepared to bushwhack and make lots of noise to announce your presence to any bears in the area. Hikers generally prefer to stay in alpine areas where the views are breathtaking and they are less likely to surprise a bear.

Be aware that walking along the old flume can be hazardous to your health as thousands of rusted nails poke out of the rotting boards. Also, water leaking out of the flume has produced a particularly vigorous shrub zone along this route. Following the rivers can be better in some spots, worse in others.

Al Aasman

High routes abound in the Tombstone region.

Hikers have also found traversing the north side of Chert Mountain quite difficult. Crossing Sheep Mountain Pass to the Little Twelve Mile River is probably a better route choice.

If you are determined to give this route a try, there are a few sites of interest along the way. See page 43 for more information on the Yukon Ditch. Following the Chandindu River tends to offer a clearer, flatter route as you must traverse across hillsides if you follow the Tombstone flume.

Look for a roofless cabin about 1 kilometre (0.6 miles) downstream of the Tombstone flume intake on a bank about 9 metres (30 ft) above the river. Ditchwalkers lived there while the flume was operating. They kept the channels clear of weeds and debris and regulated the water levels.

In 1997 a major landslide destroyed most of a maintenance camp located at the confluence of the Tombstone River and the second creek west of Horsetrack Creek, known as Number 3 Creek. Only a bathhouse, complete with a carved wooden bathtub, is left. The bathhouse walls are made of flattened kerosene cans nailed to a wooden frame.

The Little Twelve Mile power plant is about 1 kilometre (0.6 miles) west of the point where the Little Twelve Mile flume joins the Tombstone flume. Follow the river to reach the power plant. The route along the flume involves bushy climbs. Look for a small cabin and a telephone booth in the power plant area, and try to imagine the days when you could actually make a telephone call from this remote location.

The east-west ridge between Yoke and Cathedral Mountains straddles what geologists call the "contact" between intrusive and sedimentary rocks. 92 million years ago, when hot magmas intruded the older sedimentary rocks, the groundwater was also heated up. It circulated through faults deep into the earth, dissolving minerals and carrying them back towards the surface. Prospectors often explore contact zones because of the mineralization usually found there. In 1997, claims were staked below Horn Mountain, located east of the Syenite Lakes. These claims set off the controversy described in the conservation section.

The Twelve Mile (or Chandindu) River valley, was traditionally used for grayling-fishing and moose-hunting. It was also a corridor to the Yukon River, and led through good sheep habitat in the Tombstone Mountains as an added bonus. This route is still a reasonable choice for winter travel.

Tombstone Flume Intake to Yoke Mountain – Round Trip Climb

Round trip:	9 km (5.6 miles)
Allow :	10 hours
Max. elevation:	2249 m (7377 feet)
Elevation gain:	1280 m (4200 ft)

This route ascends the prominent ridge above the flume intake, but only hikers confident on steep talus slopes should attempt this climb. You can also ascend the peak from Syenite Pass, described below. The magnificent views from Yoke Mountain make the effort worthwhile.

Tombstone Flume Intake to Syenite Pass – Round Trip Hike

Round trip:	11 km (7 miles)
Allow:	8 hours
Max. elevation:	1650 m (5400 ft)
Elevation gain:	670 m (2700 ft)

Syenite Pass is the lowest and easiest route across the rampart of the Cloudy Range. But even if you are not crossing between the Tombstone and Blackstone drainages, the two Syenite Lakes are well worth a visit. Another guide book author describes them as two of the prettiest lakes in the territory.

The two Syenite Lakes are a scenic highlight of the Cloudy Range.

To reach the pass, follow the tributary that flows into the Tombstone River from the north, across from the flume intake. Part way up, start following the west side of the creek in order to avoid the heavy brush and gorges. Higher up, fantastic-looking pinnacles and spires tower above the west side of the creek.

Climbing the south side of Syenite Pass is relatively easy. On your way up, you pass a 7 metre (23 ft) high pingo. A rock glacier is visible up the slopes to the east.

From Syenite Pass you can ascend a ridge to Yoke Mountain. Descending the steep north side of Syenite Pass could be difficult under wet conditions as large boulders cover the slope. There are remnants of two glaciers north of the pass.

Upper and Lower Syenite Lakes are set in high cirques on the north side of the pass. Please tread lightly on the fragile alpine tundra surrounding them, and camp on the dry hummocky areas. Waterfalls can be found in the drainage below the lakes.

There are many beautiful lakes in this region, so consider allowing time to explore the surrounding area. To the east, a short side-trip takes you to a lovely valley in which a small waterfall plunges over polished rocks. A longer side trip could be made to Azure Lake by descending to the main drainage of the Blackstone River, hiking along its east side to Azure Creek, and following it to Azure Lake.

You can also reach the headwaters of the East Blackstone watershed by crossing a saddle on the ridge due north of Azure Lake. Rock outcrops punctuate the hillsides of this alpine valley. The sheep and caribou trails found everywhere make for easy hiking along the ridges.

Syenite Pass north to Dempster Highway
via Foxy Creek

One way:	30 kilometres
Allow:	Three days
Max. elevation:	1645 m (5400 ft)
Elevation loss:	1160 m (3800 ft)
Elevation gain:	400 m (1300 ft)

From Syenite Lakes, descend Hammer Creek to the main drainage of the Blackstone River. Travel north along this classic glacial valley to Arrow Creek. A well-traveled horse trail follows the Blackstone River for most of the route. The going is relatively easy, but the trail wanders back and forth across the river many times.

Turn east at Arrow Creek, which is about 20 kilometres from lower Syenite Lake. Blackstone Mountain, above the headwaters of Arrow Creek, has outcrops of volcanic rocks. They were formed when alkaline basalt erupted through cracks in the sea floor 450 million years ago.

Continue for about five kilometres to Auston Pass. Dall sheep and Golden Eagles' nests can often be seen around the high grassy pass. This area also gives you an enticing view down the Blackstone River valley. From the pass descend to Foxy Creek and travel east to the highway, a distance of about another 10 kilometres. As you near the highway, the valley bottom is braided with trails so try to stay on the most major ones. This route would also be good for a ski trip.

The basecamp for Pete Jensen Outfitting is located across the highway from the trailhead. While in the area, please respect the outfitters' livelihood and leave everything as found. Also be aware that hunting season usually begins in August. Check to make sure that the opening date has not changed, and wear bright colours during hunting season.

Juri Peepre

The Dempster Highway traverses one of the North's most unique landscapes.

conservation
ISSUES

THE CONSERVATION STORY BEHIND TOMBSTONE MOUNTAIN

> "Everything grows there. You have everything you want there. There's all kinds of berries, fish and little animals that live in that country. I was born and raised there in that country. That's my university."

Elder Percy Henry, Tr'ondëk Hwëch'in

Tombstone Mountain and the Blackstone Uplands have been important to aboriginal people for a very long time. In the early 1990s, when Steve Taylor was Chief of the Tr'ondëk Hwëch'in, he referred to these mountains as sacred, and stated that his people wanted a park for all Canadians. A hundred and fifty years ago First Nations people could not have imagined that it would take two decades of struggle to protect these lands and waters —an effort caught up in competing values and a colonial federal administration.

Plans to protect Tombstone Mountain began with the construction of the Dempster Highway. At that time, the Blackstone Uplands and the North Fork Pass area were traversed only by trails. In the early1970s, the Yukon government identified a small rectangular-shaped Park Reserve in the vicinity of the mountain.

In those days, parks were often created to protect beautiful scenery and recreation features, and the Tombstone story was no different. The Park Reserve around the dramatic mountains at the headwaters of the Klondike River offered no legal protection.

This early government proposal gathered dust until the Tr'ondëk Hwëch'in First Nation began negotiating their land claim in the 1980s. They recognised the importance of protecting the Tombstone Mountain area and proposed creating a territorial park as part of their land claim. The First Nation's proposals were at least twice the size of the Park Reserve identified by the Yukon government. Later, government researchers confirmed that much of the most important wildlife habitat, unusual plant species and interesting permafrost landforms were north of Tombstone Mountain in the Cloudy Range and Blackstone Uplands.

In the early 1990s the Tr'ondëk Hwëch'in were close to concluding an agreement that would have protected more than 80,000 hectares of critical wildlands when there was a change in government. To put things in perspective, Kluane National Park is more than two million hectares, so the First Nation was asking to protect an area about 3.6 percent the size of Kluane. The next Yukon administration, led by John Ostashek, would not consider the larger protected area proposal and held firm at a size of about 38,000 hectares –an area about the size of the original Park Reserve–that missed most of the important wildlife habitat.

Neither the First Nation nor the Yukon public accepted this arbitrary limit on the size of the park. Steve Taylor, then chief of the Tr'ondëk Hwëch'in, showed his dissatisfaction with this reduction in size. He said, "We want a larger park, not only to protect the plants and animals, but we want to have a park that's of significant size and importance for all Yukoners and all Canadians."

The Yukon government of the day did, however, withdraw the small core area from further mineral claim staking. This was made easier after the mining company, Archer Cathro, voluntarily relinquished its existing claims near Tombstone Mountain.

By this time the government's own scientific reports showed beyond any doubt that a small park of 38,000 hectares would do little to protect wildlife populations such as Dall sheep or the region's nine diverse ecosystem types, rare plants, subarctic birds or archaeological sites. It was obvious that a larger park was needed to keep this area truly wild and ecologically healthy. Yukoners had to choose what Tombstone Mountain would stand for in the future. Would it grace a meaningful and rich park that protects wild species, their habitat and our cultural heritage? Or would it stand as a reminder of what might have been?

A public campaign in support of the Tr'ondëk Hwëch'in efforts to protect the region began in earnest in 1994. The public clearly wanted to protect a large area in the Tombstone region, and the Yukon Chapter of the Canadian Parks and Wilderness Society (CPAWS) soon gathered more than 1,000 signatures on a petition to prove the point.

CPAWS, in affiliation with World Wildlife Fund's Endangered Spaces Campaign and its Yukon Wildlands Project partners, led the public drive. The campaign produced continued public support for a large park during the 1996 election. CPAWS called for the immediate protection of a core area of at least 100,000 hectares in the vicinity of Tombstone Mountain, with provisions to protect a further

Marten Berkman

First Nation drummers at a show of support for the Tombstones held in the Yukon Legislature.

100,000 hectares of critical habitat to the north in the Cloudy Range and Blackstone Uplands.

Protection of the Tombstone region became an election issue and all the parties were asked to commit to a larger park. The large majority of candidates for the Yukon legislature affirmed the idea and soon the park proposal became a political promise.

During the time leading up to the election, land claims negotiations with the Tr'ondëk Hwëch'in stalled because the First Nation was steadfast in its resolve to create a large and enduring park. After the election, Tombstone Mountain was often mentioned as the future "flagship" of the territorial park system. But the mining industry had a different idea about the future of this area.

While the government was considering the merits of withdrawing the proposed protected area from mineral claim staking, mining companies were out hammering claim posts in the ground. The initial claims were staked in a series of blocks in the heart of the proposed protected area, followed by further staking through the fall of 1997 in the larger park study area.

This claim staking in the area promised as a park shows how archaic mining laws based on the "free entry" mining system continue to confound the public will for conservation. For more than 70 years, "free entry" has meant that a mining company can hammer claim posts into the ground almost anywhere in the Yukon and assert that its interests take precedence over other land uses. No other industry or organization has this power. Loggers cannot stake a claim and cut trees. Wilderness tourism operators cannot stake a claim and build a fishing lodge. Conservationists cannot stake a claim and proclaim a protected area.

Recent changes to the Yukon's mining laws do nothing to address the fundamental flaw that is inherent in the "free entry" system. Conservation groups are working to change these antiquated laws and put mining on an even footing with other uses of the land.

Yukon Government

Stone point

Even after the public reacted with anger to the staking of mineral claims in the proposed Tombstone Park, the Yukon Government continued to stall.

Finally the government leader, Piers McDonald, asked the federal government to remove part of the proposed protected area— about 80,000 hectares—from any more claim staking. After two decades of talk, at least the heart of the Tombstone ecosystem was given interim protection. Even so, the future of the mining claims inside this core park area remained in doubt.

As part of the deal to withdraw the 80,000 hectare core area of the park from mineral claim staking, the Yukon government also identified a larger park study area of an additional

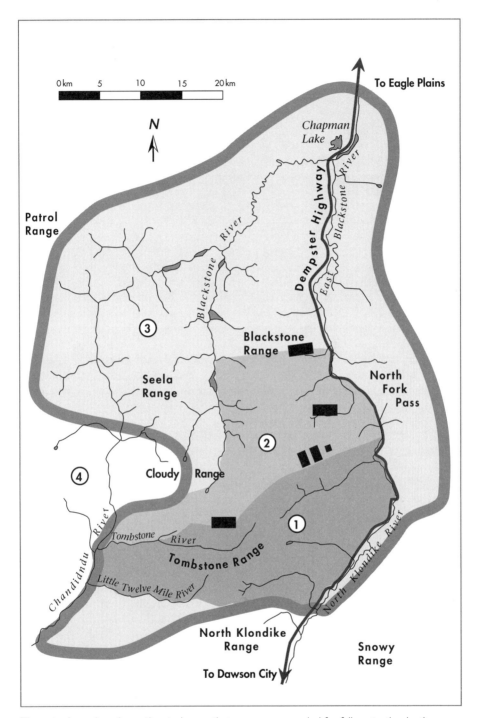

The outer boundary shows the study area that was recommended for full protection by the Tombstone Park Steering Committee. The Committee recommended a Territorial Park of more than 220,000 hectares.

150,000 hectares. This outer area was left vulnerable to more mineral claim staking, confounding future efforts to establish a park free of industrial development.

In October 1997, the Tr'ondëk Hwëch'in successfully negotiated their land claim agreement with the territorial and federal governments. Protection of an enlarged Tombstone Park was a key part of the agreement and brought to an end more than twenty years of debate about whether and how to protect the area. The agreement provided for a Steering Committee to recommend the final park boundaries.

In his budget address on February 23, 1998, Yukon Government Leader Piers McDonald agreed that the "Tombstone area along the Dempster Highway is without doubt one of the most scenic wilderness areas in the world." He went on to say that "Our government moved decisively to ensure interim protection of that area from development," and that Tombstone Park would be a "key element of the environmental legacy we will leave for generations to come."

After the land claim agreement was ratified in the fall of 1998, the Tombstone Steering Committee appointed by the Tr'ondëk Hwëch'in and the Yukon government went to work. It held a series of public meetings to review scientific and traditional knowledge about the Tombstone region.

Many people thought that the mining claims inside the proposed park would quietly disappear. After all the government's promises, it was hard to comprehend that mining exploration would be allowed in the heart of the proposed park. The public assumed that Yukon and Canada would honour the spirit of the land claim agreement and either stop work on the claims or extinguish them with some form of compensation for work completed.

These assumptions were wrong. Neither the Yukon nor federal governments acted to uphold the conservation objective of the land claim agreement, instead watching as the mining company worked its claims, perched high beneath a peak less than five kilometres away from Tombstone Mountain.

MAP EXPLANATION

Area 1   shows the original size of the park proposal
Area 2   shows the expanded area, protected from further mineral claim staking, but only after claim blocks shown in black were staked
Area 3   shows the rest of the 230,000 hectare Study Area assessed by the Tombstone Steering Committee
Area 4   shows the bite taken out of the study area by the Yukon Government due to existing mineral deposits

████   Location of mining claims staked in the proposed protected area

Late in the spring of 1999, Canadian United Minerals Inc. applied for a mining land use permit and a water licence that would have allowed them to excavate test pits half the size of a football field inside the park.

These kinds of activities in the park area are contrary to the spirit of the Tr'ondëk Hwëch'in land claim agreement, which states that the area shall be managed in accordance with conservation objectives.

Canadian United withdrew its applications, but continued work during the summer of 1999, as is allowed under Yukon mining regulations. Incredibly, in a media interview a senior federal official was quoted as supporting mining in the park as a compatible land use. CPAWS later received a clarification from then federal Department of Indian Affairs and Northern Development (DIAND) Minister Jane Stewart who said that the federal government "supports both the Yukon Protected Areas Strategy and the Whitehorse Mining Initiative." The WMI – signed by the mining industry, governments and conservationists in 1992 – calls for a system of core protected areas free of industrial development.

Yukon Government

Lichens are an important food for caribou.

The Liberal Party jumped into the fray late in the game, issuing a press release in May 1999: "By failing to ask to have land withdrawn from staking, for the proposed expansion of Tombstone, the NDP has brought us to the point where we have legitimate claims and a potential mine in this area. Despite a 1000 name petition and a lot of flowery prose …about saving park land it took the government seven months to ask for the land to be withdrawn."

During all the political scuffling, the Tombstone Park Steering Committee went about the business of reviewing the evidence and consulting the public on park boundaries. After six months of study, they released their recommendations on October 1, 1999.

The Committee heard the evidence, but also followed their hearts in calling for a park of 223,000 hectares – almost the whole study area. Finally, the years of effort by the Tr'ondëk Hwëch'in, concerned citizens, scientists and conservation organizations was drawing to a close.

The mining industry cried foul and some folks said that the park was too large. But the public mood was different. In support of the Committee's work, CPAWS and the Yukon Conservation Society held a public rally in the Yukon Government legislative building. Among the 200 people who came to show their support, were the Tr'ondëk Hwëch'in and politicians from two of the parties. Elder Percy Henry and Deputy Chief Clara Van Bibber spoke with passion about why their people sought to protect this special land.

On December 9, the Yukon government announced their decision to establish a 216,400 hectare Tombstone Territorial Park – a move that was applauded by most Yukon people.

After years of tough negotiations, public debate and political promises, the campaign to save the Tombstone Range and the Blackstone Uplands was over. Well, not quite. CPAWS warned that the Yukon and federal governments were ducking their responsibilities on the mining claims in the park.

In January 2000, Canadian United Minerals confirmed its plans to go ahead with an advanced mining exploration program on its claims in the park. The company's long range plans include a 46-kilometre road through the heart of the park, alongside the Blackstone River.

Then, in early March 2000, an unexpected announcement by federal DIAND Minister, Bob Nault, appeared to effectively put an end to the prospect of an open mine pit in the heart of Tombstone Park. In speaking to Whitehorse reporters, the Minister said, "...it is very difficult to comprehend how we can have mining in a park." He went on to say, "...we have signaled that we would like to see the whole issue of mining itself rectified and the permit situation stopped."

To the thousands of supporters of an intact Tombstone Park, the Minister's statement came as welcome news. Many people sent letters to Nault thanking him for his leadership in breaking through the stalemate. As this book goes to press, the final outcome is not yet known, but there is a mood of cautious optimism. Until the federal Minister's wishes are carried out to secure the future of the park, though, mining and industrial roads could still permanently scar the landscape.

Yukon Government/Catherine Kennedy

Rock glaciers creep downhill on cushions of ice.

Tony Gonda

Heart of the Tombstone Range.

yukon
WILDLANDS PROJECT

Protected areas safeguard only about three percent of the world's rich biological diversity. Many of these areas are home to communities of people with traditional cultures and a vital knowledge of nature. Despite the establishment of parks across North and Central America, wild nature and its dependent species are in precipitous decline.

Core protected areas alone are not enough to save biological diversity. Wildlife habitat must be cared for everywhere, and wildlife corridors must be protected to maintain connections between protected areas. A field of science called Conservation Biology, when combined with traditional ecological knowledge, gives us a way of studying and protecting ecosystems without becoming overwhelmed by the problems. The basic goals of Conservation Biology as related to protected areas and the lands around them are simple. You must:

- think big,
- think connected,
- think whole.

Most early parks in Canada were selected for scenery and recreation, or simply because they contained few extractable resources. As a result, high elevation "rocks and ice," and other pretty but not always diverse lands, dominate our system of protected areas. Many ecosystem types are not represented. Most protected areas are incomplete ecosystems, and many are islands in a sea of developed lands. It is a sad irony of our time that many large mammal species have been eliminated inside our so-called protected areas, because they cannot survive in these remnant island habitats.

The Yukon Wildlands Project is part of a North America-wide strategy to stop the disappearance of wildlife and the wild places upon which they depend. In every region of the continent, grassroots organizations are working to preserve vanishing biological diversity. In Canada, the Endangered Spaces campaign, led by the World Wildlife Fund, aims to set aside a representative part of each natural region. The Yukon Wildlands Project and the Endangered Spaces campaign goals go hand in hand.

For the past several years, the Yukon Wildlands Project and the Endangered Spaces Campaign have been a co-operative effort of the Canadian Parks and Wilderness Society-Yukon Chapter, the Yukon Conservation Society, and Friends of Yukon Rivers. CPAWS –Yukon managed the Endangered Spaces Campaign for World Wildlife Fund Canada.

YELLOWSTONE TO YUKON CONSERVATION INITIATIVE

The Yellowstone to Yukon Conservation Initiative is a bold and far-reaching vision to protect and conserve natural ecosystems along the entire length of the great mountain chain from the Rockies to the Mackenzie, Selwyn and other sister ranges of the North. If we are serious about the conservation of wildlife, we need to think at a large scale that will take care of the needs of wide-ranging species such as caribou, grizzly bear and migratory birds. Wildlife simply can not survive in small islands of protected areas alone – we need to plan for conservation throughout the landscape.

The Yellowstone to Yukon vision includes people. It embraces communities, respects traditional activities, and seeks to find ways of making room for people, wildlife and wild lands in the region.

The Yellowstone to Yukon Conservation Initiative (Y2Y) is a network of people working together to help protect wildlife and the habitat they depend upon. Y2Y is not a government plan – it is a co-operative effort between people who share the idea that protected areas and wildlife conservation in the western mountains is essential to maintain healthy ecosystems and our quality of life. The network promotes the Y2Y vision and it enables and inspires grassroots conservation groups and other organizations. Y2Y allows us to do together what we can't do alone. Local efforts become regional co-operation; regional become national; and national become international.

Yukon Wildlands Project

Winter travel

THE ENDANGERED SPACES CAMPAIGN

World Wildlife Fund and CPAWS launched the Endangered Spaces Campaign in 1989 to help conserve Canada's biodiversity. The overall goal is to complete a national network of protected areas across the country. This campaign seeks to protect an ecologically representative example of each of the country's terrestrial and marine regions.

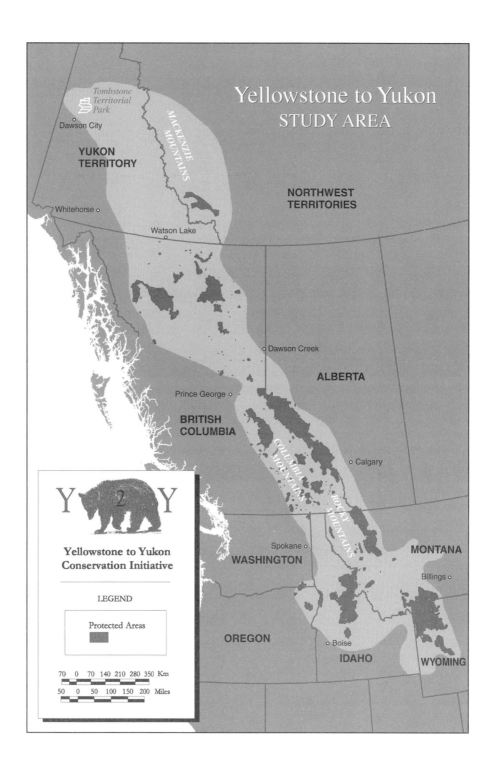

Yellowstone to Yukon
STUDY AREA

Tombstone
Territorial
Park

Dawson City

YUKON
TERRITORY

MACKENZIE
MOUNTAINS

NORTHWEST
TERRITORIES

Whitehorse

Watson Lake

Dawson Creek

ALBERTA

Prince George

BRITISH
COLUMBIA

COLUMBIA
MOUNTAINS

Calgary

ROCKY
MOUNTAINS

Y 2 Y

Yellowstone to Yukon
Conservation Initiative

LEGEND

Protected Areas

70 0 70 140 210 280 350 Km
50 0 50 100 150 200 Miles

Spokane

WASHINGTON

MONTANA

Billings

OREGON

Boise

IDAHO

WYOMING

Throughout its duration the Endangered Spaces campaign has received overwhelming support. All of Canada's federal, provincial and territorial governments have committed to the campaign goals. The Canadian Chamber of Commerce, the Canadian Bar Association and more than 300 non-governmental organizations have endorsed the campaign. More than 600,000 people have signed the Canadian Wilderness Charter, the Endangered Spaces mission statement.

The campaign has already seen the protection of hundreds of wilderness areas, including the Northern Rockies, Tatshenshini and Khutzeymateen wilderness areas in British Columbia; Wapusk National Park in Manitoba; the expansion of Wabakimi Provincial Park in Ontario; and 31 new protected areas in Nova Scotia. Tombstone Mountain will be among the Yukon territorial protected areas to be established since the start of the campaign.

In the past many parks and protected areas were selected mostly because of their scenery or unique features. The Endangered Spaces Campaign uses a science-informed approach to help select candidate protected areas. The Yukon and the rest of Canada have an astounding array of habitats. With so much diversity, how do we know where protected areas are needed? We try to meet this challenge with a scientific approach in combination with traditional and local ecological knowledge for picking candidate areas.

The primary goal of the Endangered Spaces Campaign is conserving the variety of life. The campaign has three basic scientific objectives in proposing and designing protected area strategies:

- to ensure ecosystem representation,
- to conserve viable populations of species,
- to sustain ecological processes.

Other important considerations include traditional ecological knowledge about an area's value, special features such as sacred places or mineral springs, and traditional use areas.

The scientific part is based on the strong bond between wild species and their habitats. By sampling each of the habitat types that make up the ecological fabric of the country, we can stitch together a quiltwork of protected areas that will include most of the species as well.

The Endangered Spaces campaign and the Yukon Protected Areas Strategy use natural regions as building blocks. These are called ecoregions, and are based on broad-scale changes in climate and landforms across the territory. Each of these natural regions is made

Yukon Government/John Meikle

Willow catkin

up of a patchwork of smaller habitat types called enduring features. This provides part of the framework for protected areas planning.

To fully represent a natural region, samples of all its enduring features should be included in protected areas. In this way the full range of habitats, and the plants and animals linked to those habitats, will be secured in a network of protected areas. For example, the kind of plants occurring on a swampy clay plain will be quite different from those on mountain slopes, even within the same region. Rock outcrops or river valleys can provide distinctive environments, each of which would be classified as a different enduring feature.

On land a framework of natural regions is well established. Each government – federal, provincial and territorial – has looked at its landscape to map large-scale areas of similar climate and landform patterns. Based on these variations, more than 400 natural regions have been defined on Canada's land base and there are 23 ecoregions in the Yukon. Tombstone Mountain is located in the Mackenzie Mountains ecoregion.

A PRIMER ON ECOLOGICAL INTEGRITY

Protected areas alone will not conserve Canada's variety of life. If they become islands of wild nature surrounded by development, many plant and animal species will have little chance for long-term survival. We need to care for all lands and waters, ensuring that there is sound management of our activities everywhere. An ecosystem has integrity when it is deemed characteristic for its natural region, including the composition and abundance of native species and biological communities, rates of change and supporting processes. In plain language, ecosystems have integrity when they have their native components (plants, animals and other organisms) and processes (such as growth and reproduction) intact. (This definition is from the final report of the Panel on the Ecologolgical Integrity of Canada's National Parks, March, 2000.) By definition, wilderness has a high degree of ecological integrity. With each loss of a native species, the integrity of the ecosystem declines.

Syenite Lake

Yukon Government/John Meikle

Protected areas work best when they are connected to healthy lands and waters. Human uses around protected areas need to be carefully managed. For example, small scale selective logging may be suitable right next to a protected area, while large-scale industrial logging may result in unacceptable impacts on the area.

"A thing is right when it tends to preserve the integrity, stability, and beauty of the biotic community. It is wrong when it tends otherwise."

Aldo Leopold, 1949

When Aldo Leopold wrote those words in 1949, he could have been describing the sorts of problems found in today's industrial landscape as well as around many protected areas. Even in the Yukon, the ecological integrity of parks such as Kluane could be adversely affected if they are surrounded by incompatible types of development.

Protected areas should be able to sustain natural processes, such as fires in the boreal forest. They should maintain or restore viable populations of wildlife, including wideranging species like caribou, and they should encourage uses that are sustainable and compatible rather than destructive.

Cottongrass

Recognized criteria for maintainging ecological integrity:

1. *Sustain natural processes, such as fire and flooding, within normal ranges of variation.*

2. *Maintain or restore viable populations of all native species.*

3. *Encourage human uses compatible with maintenance of ecological integrity.*

This is no easy task, particularly when humans change the natural landscape around a protected area. If we want to keep species from going extinct, we have to pay close attention to the design and management of protected areas. They must be in the right place, and of the right size and shape, to help protect biodiversity in the long run.

When drawing boundaries for protected areas, one of the key questions to ask is "How much habitat do we need to maintain a viable population of a particular species over time." Fragmenting habitat is one of the surest ways to harm the ecological integrity of an area.

Species have different needs, so biologists often focus on umbrella species such as grizzly bears. Grizzlies and other large carnivores need large areas of undeveloped land for survival. If we provide enough secure habitat for these animals at the top of the food chain, it is assumed that most of the species further down will survive as well. In other words, if we protect grizzly habitat, we set up an umbrella for protecting other species as well.

Just as there are different types of protected areas, there are different ways to manage them. In some critical wildlife areas, there might be limits on public hunting and fishing. In others, motorized vehicles might not be appropriate. In some places, recreational use might be carefully managed to protect a special cultural or archeological site.

TOMBSTONE MOUNTAIN AND THE MACKENZIE MOUNTAINS ECOREGION

The Mackenzie Mountains, one of the Yukon's largest and most diverse ecoregions extends from the rugged Mackenzie ranges in the Northwest Territories, through the

Arctic Terns

Yukon Government

Yukon's Wernecke and South Ogilvie Mountains almost to the Alaskan Border. In the original ecoregion mapping by Oswald and Senyk in 1977, this region was divided into two areas that separated out the south Ogilive Mountains. This division reflected the different conditions found in the western Tombstone area compared to the forested Snake and Bonnet Plume River valleys along the NWT border. Although both areas are now lumped into one ecoregion, they include very different landscape conditions.

The Tombstone Mountain park area does not adequately represent the ecoregion as a whole, but is important for its many special ecological and cultural features. More large protected areas are needed in the eastern half of the Mackenzie Mountains ecoregion, for example in the Snake River and the Bonnet Plume River watersheds. The latter has been designated a Canadian Heritage River.

ROADS AND WILDERNESS

There can be no doubt that both mineral exploration and operating mines have an impact on wildlife and wildlife habitat. The roads that development brings are arguably an equally important issue.

Before the Second World War and the building of the Alaska Highway there were no roads in the Yukon. Over the last half a century, a web of roads has spread across the territory. The Yukon now has more than 5,000 kilometres of roads, and at least another 5,000 kilometres of vehicle-access routes. The cumulative effect on wildlife of increased access into wild lands has been detrimental to many species such as woodland caribou.

We live in a society obsessed with "access"; especially that fast, easy access that roads can provide. But roads do more than just provide access, they degrade and destroy ecosystems.

An overwhelming body of scientific information explains how and why roads disrupt ecological ecosystems. They deliver massive quantities of sediment to streams, disrupt hydrologic cycles by altering runoff patterns and intercepting subsurface flows, reduce and fragment wildlife habitat and introduce exotic species. In more visible ways, they provide the means for massive numbers of road kills each year. Roads and associated developments almost always result in increased hunting and decline of wildlife populations.

More Ghost Roads Mean Declining Wildlife

In the U.S., Forest Service studies show that less than half of road closures are effective in keeping motorized vehicles off the closed roads. Only half of the habitat within roaded areas is considered secure from the negative influence of road-related human activities.

In the Yukon, road access has been clearly linked to declines in wildlife populations due to over-hunting. For example, the ratio of cow moose to calves in the Kluane region is much healthier in areas without road access than areas with easy road access. Sheep ratios show a similar pattern.

Woodland Caribou At Risk

Road access and development harms wood-land caribou herds and displaces wilderness dependent species such as grizzly bears and wolverines. Excessive road networks make it easier for predators such as wolves to hunt woodland caribou.

Ken Madsen

Both woodland and barrenground caribou make their homes in this region.

In the Yukon there are only a few large mammal ecosystems dominated by woodland caribou herds that have not been affected by roads, development, intense hunting and man-agement intervention – these include the Wolf Lake and Bonnet Plume caribou herds. We don't know all that is needed to save woodland caribou herds, so we need to be conser-vative and ensure that we retain some herds within intact ecosystems.

Roads:

- fragment wildlife habitat and cause the decline of many species,
- create barriers to the movement of wide-ranging species such as caribou and grizzlies,
- make over-hunting and poaching possible,
- encourage more road building and allow for increased access for all-terrain vehicles.

WE NEED YOUR SUPPORT TO CARRY OUT OUR YUKON WORK

We will welcome your support through membership or volunteer help with projects and events.

Canadian Parks and Wilderness Society
Yukon Chapter (CPAWS–Yukon)
P.O. Box 31095
Whitehorse, YT Y1A 5P7

Phone:	867-393-8080
Fax:	867-393-8081

Web Site:	http://www.cpaws.org
	(With a link to the CPAWS–Yukon Chapter)
E-mail:	cpaws@yknet.yk.ca

World Wildlife Fund Canada

For information on Yukon issues, contact the Yukon's World Wildlife Fund regional co-operator, CPAWS–Yukon, above.

For national information, contact:

World Wildlife Fund
245 Eglinton Ave East, Suite 410
Toronto, ON M4P 3J1

Phone:	416-489-4567
Fax:	416-489-3611
Toll Free:	1-800-26-PANDA

Web Site:	http://www.wwfcanada.org
E-mail:	panda@wwfcanada.org

OTHER ORGANIZATIONS

Yukon Conservation Society
P.O. Box 4163
Whitehorse, YT Y1A 3S9

Phone:	867-668-5678
Fax:	867-668-6637
E-mail:	ycs@polarcom.com

appendix A

BIRDS IN THE TOMBSTONE AREA

Red-throated Loon
Pacific Loon
Common Loon
Horned Grebe
Red-necked Grebe
Tundra Swan
Trumpeter Swan
Snow Goose (rare)
Brant (very rare)
Greater White-fronted Goose
Canada Goose
Green-winged Teal

Mallard Duck
Northern Pintail
Blue-winged Teal
Northern Shoveler
Gadwall
American Wigeon
Eurasian Wigeon (rare)
Canvasback
Redhead
Ringed-necked Duck
Lesser Scaup
Greater Scaup

Harlequin Duck
Oldsquaw
Surf Scoter
White-winged Scoter
Common Goldeneye
Barrow's Goldeneye
Bufflehead
Common Merganser
Red-breasted Merganser
Bald Eagle
Golden Eagle
Northern Harrier
Sharp-shinned Hawk
Northern Goshawk
Red-tailed Hawk
Rough-legged Hawk
American Kestrel
Merlin
Peregrine Falcon
Gyrfalcon
Spruce Grouse
Willow Ptarmigan
Rock Ptarmigan
White-tailed Ptarmigan
Ruffed Grouse
Sharp-tailed Grouse
Spruce Grouse
Sandhill Crane

WWF

Red-throated Loon

American Golden-Plover
Killdeer
Semipalmated Plover
Lesser Yellowlegs
Solitary Sandpiper
Wandering Tattler
Spotted Sandpiper
Upland Sandpiper
Whimbrel
Surfbird
Semipalmated Sandpiper
Least Sandpiper
Baird's Sandpiper
Pectoral Sandpiper
Stilt Sandpiper (rare)
Buff-breasted Sandpiper
(rare)
Hudsonian Godwit (rare)
Long-billed Dowitcher
Common Snipe
Red-necked Phalarope
Parasitic Jaeger (very rare)
Long-tailed Jaeger
Bonaparte's Gull
Herring Gull
Glaucous Gull (rare)
Mew Gull
Arctic Tern
Great Horned Owl
Northern Hawk-Owl
Great Gray Owl
Short-eared Owl
Boreal Owl
Belted Kingfisher
Hairy Woodpecker
Three-toed Woodpecker
Northern Flicker
Olive-sided Flycatcher
Alder Flycatcher
Least Flycatcher
Say's Phoebe
Horned Lark

Tree Swallow
Violet-green Swallow
Bank Swallow
Cliff Swallow
Gray Jay
Black-billed Magpie
Common Raven
Black-capped Chickadee
Boreal Chickadee
American Dipper
Northern Wheatear
Townsend's Solitaire
Gray-cheeked Thrush
Swainson's Thrush
Hermit Thrush
American Robin
Varied Thrush
Ruby-crowned Kinglet
American Pipit
Bohemian Waxwing
Northern Shrike
Orange-crowned Warbler
Yellow Warbler
Yellow-rumped Warbler
Townsend's Warbler

Blackpoll Warbler
Northern Waterthrush
Common Yellowthroat
Wilson's Warbler
Rusty Blackbird
Gray-crowned Rosy Finch
Pine Grosbeak
White-winged Crossbill
Common Redpoll
Hoary Redpoll
Pine Siskin
American Tree Sparrow
Savannah Sparrow
Fox Sparrow
Lincoln's Sparrow
Golden-crowned Sparrow
Dark-eyed Junco
Lapland Longspur
Snow Bunting

Jim Hawkings

Goslings

appendix B

PLANTS IN THE TOMBSTONE AREA

This is a checklist of plants that are likely to be encountered in the Tombstone Ranges and Blackstone Uplands. From Kennedy and Smith (1999); Trelawney (1988)

Achillea millefolium L.
Common Yarrow

Achillea sibirica Ledeb.
Siberian Yarrow

Aconitum delphinifolium DC.
Northern Monkshood

Adoxa moschatellina L.
Moschatel

Alnus crispa (Drylander ex Ait) Pursh
Mountain Alder

Alnus incana (L.)
Grey Alder

Alyssum americanum Greene
Alyssum

Andromeda polifolia L.
Bog Rosemary

Androsace chamaejasme Wulf.
Rock Jasmine

Anemone drummondii Wats.
Alpine Anemone

Anemone narcissiflora L.
Narcissus-flowered Anemone

Anemone parviflora Michx.
Northern Anemone

Anemone richardsonii Hook.
Yellow Anemone

Antennaria rosea Greene
Pink Pussy-toes

Arabis drummondii Gray
Rock Cress

Arctostaphylos alpina (L.) Spreng.
Alpine Bearberry

Arctostaphylos rubra (Rehd. & Wils.) Fern.
Red Bearberry

Arnica angustifolia Vahl.
Alpine Arnica

Arnica lessingii Greene
Lessing's Arnica

Artemisia alaskana Rydb.
Alaska Wormwood

Artemisia tilesii Ledeb.
Mountain Wormwood

Aster alpinus L.
Montain Aster

Aster sibericus L.
Siberian Aster

Astragalus alpinus L.
Alpine Milk-vetch

Astragalus umbellatus Bunge
Hairy Arctic Milk-vetch

Barbarea orthoceras Ledeb.
Winter Cress

Betula glandulosa Michx.
Dwarf Birch

Betula occidentalis Hook.
Water Birch

Betula papyrifera Marsh.
Paper Birch

Boschniakia rossica (Cham. & Schlecht.) Fedtsch.
Ground Cone

Boykinia richardsonii (Hook.) A. Gray
Alaska Boykinia

Caltha palustris L. ssp. *arctica* (R. Br.) Huth.
Marsh Marigold

Campanula aurita Greene
Yukon Bellflower

Campanula lasiocarpa Cham.
Alpine Harebell

Campanula uniflora L.
Arctic Harebell

Cardamine bellidifolia L.
Alpine Bittercress

Jennifer Staniforth

Northern shooting star
(*Dodecatheon frigidum*)

Cardamine pratensis L.
Cuckoo Flower

Cardamine purpurea Cham.
& Schlecht.
Purple Cress

Cassiope tetragona (L.) D.
Don
White Mountain Heather

Castilleja caudata (Pennell)
Rebr.
Pale Paintbrush

Castilleja hyperborea Pennell
Northern Paintbrush

Castilleja yukonis Pennell
Yukon Paintbrush

Cerastium beeringianum
Cham. & Schlecht.
Mouse-ear Chickweed

Chrysosplenium wrightii
Franch. & Sav.
Golden Saxifrage

Claytonia tuberosa Pall.
Tuberous Spring-beauty

Cornus canadensis L.
Bunchberry

Corydalis pauciflora (Steph.)
Pers.
Few-flowered Corydalis

Corydalis sempervirens (L.)
Pers.
Pink Corydalis

Crepis nana Richards.
Dwarf Hawk's-beard

Delphinium glaucum Wats.
Tall Delphinium

Descurainia sophioides
(Fisch.) O.E. Schulz
Tansy Mustard

Dodecatheon frigidum Cham.
& Schlecht.
Northern Shooting Star

Douglasia gormanii
Constance
Douglasia

Draba alpina L.
Alpine Draba

Draba ogilviensis Hult.
Ogilvie Draba

Dryas alaskensis A.E. Porsild
Mountain Avens (4 species)

Empetrum nigrum L.
Crowberry

Epilobium angustifolium L.
Fireweed

Epilobium latifolium L.
Broad-leaved Fireweed

Epilobium palustre L.
Swamp Willow-herb

Erigeron acris L.
Fleabane Daisy

Erigeron humilis Graham
Mountain Fleabane

Erigeron purpuratus Greene
Arctic Fleabane

Eritrichium aretioides
(Cham. & Schlecht.) DC.
Arctic Forget-me-not

Erysimum pallasii (Pursh)
Fern.
Pallas' Wallflower

Galium boreale L.
Northern Bedstraw

Gentiana algida Pall.
Whitish Gentian

Gentiana glauca Pall.
Glaucous Gentian

Gentiana propinqua
Richards.
Four-petalled Gentian

Gentiana prostrata Haenke
Moss Gentian

Geocaulon lividum
(Richards.) Fern
Northern Comandra

Hedysarum alpinum L.
Bear Root
Alpine Sweet-vetch

Heracleum lanatum Michx.
Cow Parsnip

Hieracium gracile Hook.
Slender Hawkweed

Hippuris vulgaris L.
Common Mare's-tail

Juniperus communis L.
Ground Juniper

Kalmia polifolia Wang. s.l.
Bog Laurel

Lagotis glauca Gaertn.
Lagotis

Ledum groenlandicum Oeder
Labrador Tea

Lepidium densiflorum
Schrad.
Common Pepper-grass

Linnaea borealis L.
Twinflower

Lloydia serotina (L.) Rchb.
Alp Lily

Loiseluria procumbens (L.)
Desv.
Alpine Azalea

Lupinus arcticus Wats.
Arctic Lupine

Menyanthes trifoliata L.
Buckbean

Mertensiana paniculata (Ait.)
G.Don
Bluebells

Minuartia arctica (Stev.)
Aschers. & Graebn.
Sandwort (6 species)

Moneses uniflora (L.) Gray
Single Delight

Montia scammaniana
(Hulten) Welsh
Montia

Myosotis alpestris Schm.
Alpine Forget-me-not

Myriophyllum sibiricum
Komarov
Water-milfoil

Nuphar polysepalum Engelm.
Yellow Water-lily

Orthilia secunda (L.) House
One-sided Wintergreen

Oxycoccus microcarpus Turcz.
Bog Cranberry

Oxyria digyna (L.) J. Hill
Mountain Sorrel

Oxytropis campestris (L.) DC.
Late Yellow Locoweed

Oxytropis deflexa (Pall.) DC.
Defelexed Oxytrope

Oxytropis maydelliana
Trautv.
Madell's Oxytrope

Oxytropis nigrescens (Pall.)
Fisch
Blackish Crazyweed

Papaver lapponicum (Tolm.)
Nordh.
Poppy

Papaver macounii Greene
Macoun's Poppy

Papaver mcconelii Hulten
McConnel's Poppy

Parnassia kotzebuei Cham. &
Schlecht.
Kotzebue Grass-of-parnassus

Parnassia palustris L.
Marsh Grass-of-parnassus

Parrya nudicaulis (L.) Regel
Parrya

Pedicularis capitata Adams
Capitate Lousewort

Pedicularis labradorica
Wirsing
Labrador Lousewort

Pedicularis lanata Cham. &
Schlecht
Woolly Lousewort

Pedicularis langsdorfii Fisch.
Langsdorf's Lousewort

Pedicularis lapponica L.
Lapland Lousewort

Pedicularis sudetica Willd.
Sudeten Lousewort

Petasites frigidus (L.) Cass
Arctic Sweet Coltsfoot

Phacelia mollis Macbr.
Hairy Scorpion-weed

Phlox alaskensis Jordal
Siberian Phlox

Phyllodoce empetriformis
(Sm.) D. Don.
Pink Mountain Heather

Picea glauca (Moench) Voss
White Spruce

Picea mariana (Mill.) B.S.P.
Black Spruce

Pinguicula villosa L.
Hairy Butterwort

Plantago major L.
Common Plantain

Platanthera obtusata (Pursh)
Lindley
Small Northern Bog Orchid

Polemonium acutiflorum
Willd.
Tall Jacob's Ladder

Polemonium boreale Adams
Northern Jacob's Ladder

Polemonium pulcherrimum
Hook.
Showy Jacob's Ladder

Polyganum alaskanum Wight
ex Hulten
Wild Rhubarb

Polygonum bistorta L.
Bistort

Polygonum viviparum L.
Alpine Bistort

Potentila hyparctica Malte
Arctic Cinquefoil

Potentilla biflora Willd.
Two-flowered Cinquefoil

Potentilla fruticosa L. ssp
floribunda (Pursh) Elkington
Shrubby Cinquefoil

Potentilla pallustris (L.) Scop.
Swamp Cinquefoil

Potentilla uniflora Ledeb.
Villous Cinquefoil

Pyrola asarifolia Michx.
Large Wintergreen

Pyrola chlorantha Sw.
Greenish-flowered
Wintergreen

Pyrola grandiflora Radius
Arctic Wintergreen

Ranunculus aquatilus L.
Water Crowfoot

Ranunculus eschscholtzii
Schlecht.
Mountain Buttercup

Ranunculus flammula L.
Creeping Spearwort

Ranunculus hyperboreus
Rottb.
Arctic Buttercup

Ranunculus nivalis L.
Snow Buttercup

Ranunculus pygmaeus
Wahlenb.
Dwarf Buttercup

Ranunculus sulphureus Sol.
Sulphur Buttercup

Rhodiola rosea L.
Roseroot

Rhododendron lapponicum
(L.) Wahlenb.
Lapland Rosebay

Ribes hudsonianum Richards.
Northern Black Currant

Ribes triste Pall.
Northern Red Currant

Rorippa barbareifolia (DC.)
Kitagawa
Yellow Cress

Rosa acicularis Lindbl.
Prickly Rose

Rubus arcticus L. ssp. *arcticus*
Dwarf Raspberry

Rubus chamaemorus L.
Cloudberry

Rubus idaeus L. s.l.
Wild Red Raspberry

Rumex arcticus Trautv.
Arctic Dock

Sagina nivalis (Lindbl.) Fries
Pearlwort

Salix (16 species)
Willow

Salix arctica Pall.
Arctic Willow

Saussurea angustifolia (Willd.) DC.
Saussurea

Saxifraga adscendens L
Wedge-leaf Saxifrage

Saxifraga caespitosa L
Tufted Saxifrage

Saxifraga cernua L.
Nodding Saxifrage

Saxifraga flagellaris Willd.
Spider Plant

Saxifraga hieracifolia Waldst. & Kit.
Stiff-stemmed Saxifrage

Saxifraga hirculus L.
Yellow Marsh Saxifrage

Saxifraga oppositifolia L.
Purple Mountain Saxifrage

Saxifraga reflexa Hook.
Yukon Saxifrage

Saxifraga serpyllifolia Pursh
Thyme-leaved Saxifrage

Saxifraga tricuspidata Rottb.
Three-toothed Saxifrage

Senecio atropurpureus (Ledeb.) Fedtsch.
Groundsel

Senecio congestus (R.Br.) DC.
Mastodon Flower

Senecio lugens Richards.
Black-tipped Groundsel

Senecio pauciflorus Pursh
Rayless Alpine Butterweed

Senecio triangularis Hook.
Arrowleaf Senecio

Senecio yukonensis Porsild
Yukon Groundsel

Shepherdia canadensis (L.) Nutt.
Soapberry

Siabbaldia procumbens L.
Sibbaldia

Silene acaulis L. ssp. *acaulis*
Moss Campion

Smelowskia calycina (Stephan) C.A. Mey. S.l.
Smelowskia

Solidago multiradiata Ait.
Northern Goldenrod

Spirawa beauverdiana Schneid.
Beauverd's Spiraea

Stellaria borealis Bigelow
Chickweed (4 species)

Synthyris borealis Pennell
Kitten Tails

Taraxacum ceratophorum (Ledeb.) DC.
Dandelion

Thalictrum alpinum L.
Arctic Meadowrue

Thalictrum sparsiflorum Turcz.
Few-flowered Meadowrue

Tofieldia coccinea Richards.
Northern False Asphodel

Tofieldia pusilla (Michx.) Pers.
Scotch Asphodel

Utricularia minor L.
Lesser Bladderwort

Vaccinium uliginosum L..
Alpine Blueberry

Vaccinium vitis-idaea L.
Lingonberry

Valeriana capitata Pall.
Capitate Valerian

Veronica wormskjoldii Roem. & Schult.
Alpine Speedwell

Viburnum edule (Michx.) Raf.
High-bush Cranberry

Viola epipsila Ledeb.
Marsh Violet

Wilhelmsia physodes (Fisch.) McNeill
Merckia

Zyadenus elegans Pursh
Elegant Poison Camas

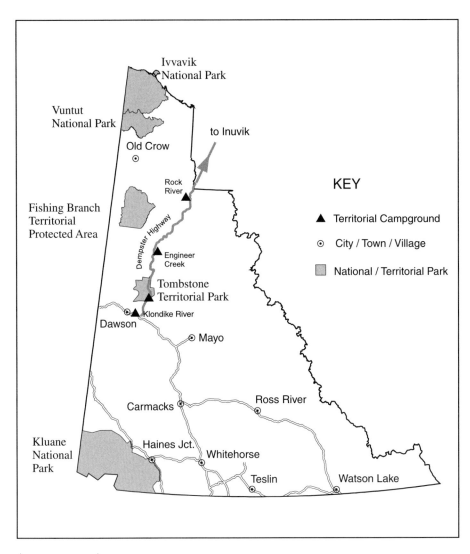

Area campgrounds

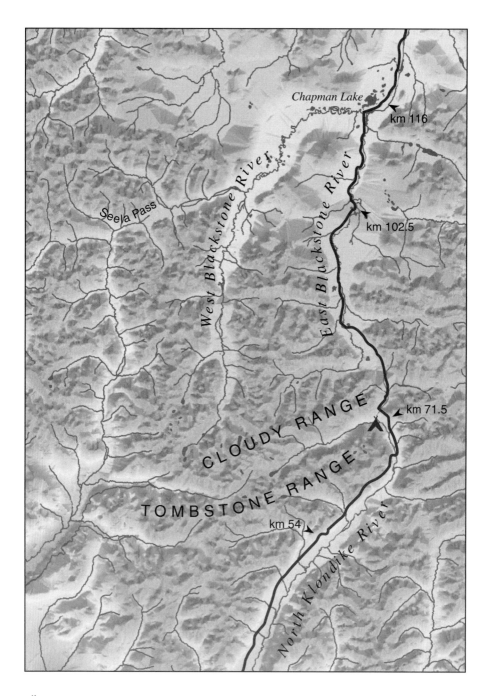

Chapman Lake

km 116

km 102.5

West Blackstone River

East Blackstone River

Seela Pass

CLOUDY RANGE

km 71.5

TOMBSTONE RANGE

km 54

North Klondike River

Ⲗ   Tombstone Territorial Park Campground

Relief map of Tombstone Range and Blackstone Uplands.

bibliography

Bird, J. Brian. 1980. *The Natural Landscapes of Canada. A Study in Regional Earth Science.* John Wiley and Sons. Toronto. ISBN 0-471-99810-9.

Bremner, T.J. 1994. *Proposed Tombstone Area Park: A Preliminary Review of Mineral Potential.* Unpublished report prepared for the Exploration and Geological Services Division, Yukon Region, Indian and Northern Affairs Canada. 115 pp.

Calef, George. 1984. *The Dempster Highway: A traveller's guide to the land and its people.* Yukon Conservation Society. Whitehorse.

Clark, Donald W. 1991. *Western Subarctic Prehistory.* Canadian Museum of Civilization. Hull, Quebec.

Cody, William J. 1996. *Flora of the Yukon Territory.* National Research Council of Canada Research Press. Ottawa. ISBN 0-660-16406-X.

Coutts, R.C. 1980. *Yukon Places and Names.* Gray's Publishing Limited. Sidney, B.C.

Danks, H.V. and J.A. Downes. 1997. *Insects of the Yukon.* Biological Survey of Canada Monograph series No. 2. Ottawa.

Ehrlich, Paul R., D. S. Dobkin and D. Wheye. 1988. *Birder's Handbook: a field guide to the natural history of North American birds.* New York: Simon & Schuster Inc.

French, H.M. and J.A. Heginbottom (eds.). 1983. *Guidebook to permafrost and related features of the northern Yukon Territory and Mackenzie Delta, Canada.* Guidebook 3. Fourth International Conference on Permafrost and International Geographical Union Commission on the significance of periglacial phenomena. University of Alaska, Fairbanks. 186 pp.

Frisch, Robert. 1987. *Birds by the Dempster Highway.* Morris Printing Company. Victoria, B.C.

Gadd, Ben. 1995. *Handbook of the Canadian Rockies.* Corax Press. Jasper, Alberta. ISBN 0-9692631-1-2.

Government of Yukon, Parks and Outdoor Recreation Branch. 1993. *Recreation Resources within the Proposed Tombstone Mountain Park.* Unpublished report. 20 pp.

_____ 1993. *Dempster Highway Travelogue.* Unpublished manuscript prepared for Dempster Highway Interpretive Center. 19 pp.

_____ 1993. *Wildlife Viewing Potential, Proposed Tombstone Park.* Yukon. Unpublished report. 6 pp.

Greer, Sheila. 1989. *Dempster Highway Corridor Human History and Heritage Resources.* Unpublished report prepared for Heritage Branch, Department of Tourism, and Department of Renewable Resources, Yukon Territorial Government. 54 pp.

Hart, C. 1998. *Geological Framework of the Yukon Territory.* Yukon Geology Program web page. www.yukonweb.com. 6 pp.

Heginbottom, J.A. 1995. *Canada – Permafrost.* National Atlas of Canada, 5th edition.

Hogan, Barbara and G. Skuce. 1993. *An Inventory and Assessment of the Historic Resources in the Proposed Tombstone Territorial Park.* Unpublished report prepared for Yukon Government. 13 pp.

Hughes, O.L. 1969. *Distribution of open-system pingos in central Yukon Territory with respect to glacial limits.* Geological Survey of Canada Paper 85-25, 19 pp.

Johnson, Derek, L. Kershaw, A. MacKinnon, and J. Pojar. 1995. *Plants of the Western Boreal Forest and Aspen Parkland.* Lone Pine Publishing. Edmonton. ISBN 1-55105-058-7.

Kennedy, Catherine E. and C.A.S. Smith. 1999. *Vegetation, terrain and natural features in the Tombstone Area, Yukon Territory.* Dept. of Renewable Resources, Government of the Yukon and Agriculture Agri-Food Canada, Whitehorse.ISBN 1-55018-913-1.

Kershaw, L. J. 1991. *The Plants of Northwestern Canada: With Special Reference to the Dempster Highway, Yukon and NWT.* Unpublished manuscript.

Madsen, Ken. 1996. *Paddling in the Yukon.* Primrose Publishing. Whitehorse, Yukon.

Lanz, Walter. 1990. *Along the Dempster: an outdoor guide to Canada's northernmost highway.* Second edition. Oak House Publishing. Vancouver.

McCandless, R.G. 1985. *Yukon Wildlife, A Social History.* University of Alberta Press.

McClellan, C. 1987. *Part of the Land, Part of the Water.* Douglas and McIntyre, Vancouver.

McPhee, John. 1998. *Annals of the Former World.* Farrar, Straus and Giroux. New York.

Oswald, E.T. and J.P. Senyk. 1977. *Ecoregions of Yukon Territory.* Publ. No. BC-X-164. Canadian Forestry Service, Pacific Forest Research Centre, Victoria, B.C. 115 pp. and map.

Peepre, J.S. and Associates. 1989. *Dempster Highway Corridor Interpretive Strategy*. Background report prepared for Yukon Territorial Government Department of Tourism and the Dempster Highway Corridor Technical Study Team.

Peepre, J.S. and Associates. 1992. *Boundary options for the Proposed Tombstone Territorial Park*. Unpublished report prepared for Parks and Recreation Section, Yukon Department of Renewable Resources, Whitehorse. 19 pp.

Permafrost Subcommittee. 1988. *Glossary of permafrost and related ground-ice terms*. National Research Council of Canada, Ottawa. Technical Memorandum No. 142, 156 pp.

Phillips, David. 1990. *Climates of Canada*. Canadian Govt. Publishing Center. Ottawa. ISSN 0-660-13459-4.

Pielou, E.C. 1991. *After the Ice Age, The Return of Life to Glaciated North America*. University of Chicago Press, Chicago.

Schofield, Janice. 1989. *Discovering Wild Plants: Alaska, Western Canada, the Northwest*. Alaska Northwest Books. Seattle.

Sherry, Erin and Vuntut Gwitch'in First Nation. 1999. *The Land Still Speaks: Gwitch'in Words about Life in Dempster Country*. Vuntut Gwitch'in First Nation. Canada.

Tarnocai, C., C.A.S. Smith and C.A. Fox. 1993. *International Tour of Permafrost Affected Soils. The Yukon and Northwest Territories of Canada*. Centre for Land and Biological Resources Research, Research Branch, Agriculture Canada, Ottawa, Canada. 197 pp.

Trelawny, John G. 1988. *Wildflowers of the Yukon, Alaska and Northwestern Canada*. Sono Nis Press. Victoria, BC. ISBN 0-919203-95-7.

Vitt, Dale H., Janet E. Marsh and Robin E. Bovey. 1988. *Mosses, Lichens and Ferns of Northwest North America*. Lone Pine Publishing. Edmonton, Alberta.

Wareham, Bill. 1991. *British Columbia Wildlife Viewing Guide*. Lone Pine Publishing. Edmonton, Alberta.

Williams, Peter J. and M.W. Smith. 1989. *The Frozen Earth: Fundamentals of Geocryology* Cambridge University Press. Cambridge, England.

Youngman, Phillip M. 1975. *Mammals of the Yukon Territory*. National Museum of Natural Sciences, Ottawa.

Yukon Wildlands Project. 1996. *Yukon Wild: Natural Regions of the Yukon*. Jasper Printing. Edmonton, Alberta.

Louise Profeit-Leblanc

Annie Henry was born in Black City and lived in the Blackstone Uplands for many years.